SERIES EDITORS

TRACY L. PELLETT   JACK RUTHERFORD   CLAUDIA BLACKMAN

Skills, Drills & Strategies for

Golf

Kenneth P. Stephens
Joni M. Stephens

Holcomb Hathaway, Publishers
Scottsdale, Arizona 85250

Library of Congress Cataloging-in-Publication Data

Stephens, Kenneth P., 1960–
    Skills, drills & strategies for golf / Kenneth P. Stephens, Joni
M. Stephens.
        p.   cm. — (The teach, coach, play series)
    Includes index.
    ISBN 1–890871–15–X
    1. Golf.   2. Golf—Training.   3. Golf—Psychological aspects.
I. Stephens, Joni M., 1961–   . II. Title.   III. Title: Skills,
drills, and strategies for golf.   IV. Title: Golf.   V. Series.
GV965.S823   1999
796.352'3—dc21   98–56208
                                                        CIP

Copyright © 1999 by Holcomb Hathaway, Inc.

 Holcomb Hathaway, Publishers, Inc.
6207 North Cattle Track Road
Scottsdale, Arizona 85250

10 9 8 7 6 5 4 3 2

ISBN 1-890871-15-X

Printed in the United States of America.

Contents

SECTION 4   Strategies   65

SECTION 5   Glossary   73

Preface

The books in the *Teach, Coach, Play* series emphasize a systematic learning approach to sports and activities. Both visual and verbal information are presented so that you can easily understand the material and improve your performance.

Built-in learning aids help you master each skill in a step-by-step manner. Using the cues, summaries, skills, drills, and illustrations will help you build a solid foundation for safe and effective participation now and in the future.

This text is designed to illustrate correct techniques and demonstrate how to achieve optimal results. Take a few minutes to become familiar with the textbook's organization and features. Knowing what to expect and where to look for material will help you get the most out of the textbook, your practice time, and this course.

TO THE INSTRUCTOR

Your needs are changing, your courses are changing, your students are changing, and the demands from your administration are changing. By setting out to create a series of books that addresses many of these changes, we've created a series that:

- Provides complete, consistent coverage of each sport—the basics through skills and drills to game strategies so you can meet the needs of majors and non-majors alike.
- Includes teaching materials so that new and recently assigned instructors have the resources they need to teach the course.
- Allows you to cover exactly the sports and activities you want with the depth of coverage you want.

What's in the *Teach, Coach, Play* Series?

- Nine Activities:
    Skills, Drills, & Strategies for Badminton
    Skills, Drills, & Strategies for Basketball
    Skills, Drills, & Strategies for Bowling
    Skills, Drills, & Strategies for Golf

Skills, Drills, & Strategies for Racquetball
Skills, Drills, & Strategies for Strength Training
Skills, Drills, & Strategies for Swimming
Skills, Drills, & Strategies for Tennis
Skills, Drills, & Strategies for Volleyball

- Accompanying instructor's manuals

What's in the Student *Teach, Coach, Play* Textbooks?

The basic approach in all of the *Teach, Coach, Play* activity titles is to help students improve their skills and performance by building mastery from simple to complex levels.

The basic organization in each textbook is as follows:

Section 1 overviews history, organizations and publications, conditioning activities, safety, warm up suggestions, and equipment.

Section 2 covers exercises or skills, participants, action involved, rules, facility or field, scoring, and etiquette.

Section 3 focuses on skills and drills or program design.

Section 4 addresses a broad range of strategies specifically designed to improve performance now and in the future.

Section 5 provides a convenient glossary of terms.

Supplements to Support You and Your Students

The *Teach, Coach, Play* books provide useful and practical instructional tools. Each activity is supported by its own manual. Each of these instructor's manuals includes classroom management notes, safety guidelines, teaching tips, ideas for inclusion of students with special needs, drills, lesson plans, evaluation notes, test bank, and a list of resources for you.

About the Authors

Kenneth P. (Pat) Stephens, a Class A PGA Professional, serves as Head Coach for the Eastern Kentucky University Men's Golf Team and Head Professional at Arlington Golf Course in Richmond, Kentucky. Pat Stephens has competed in golf at many levels, having played golf for Madison Central High School, the University of Kentucky, and Eastern Kentucky University. He was a high school All American, then went on to lead his college team at EKU to two Ohio Valley Conference Championships. After college, Stephens played on several mini-tours throughout the South before becoming a PGA Professional. He has had numerous golf accomplishments during his golf career, including qualifying for the 1988 U.S. Open, qualifying for the National PGA Club Professional Championships four of the last six years, and being named 1996 Kentucky PGA Player of the Year and Merchandiser of the Year for Public Courses. He has also recently been named to the Ohio Valley Conference All-Time Golf Team.

Joni M. Stephens is an Assistant Professor of Physical Education and Head Coach for the Eastern Kentucky University Women's Golf Team. She had a successful high school athletic career, then went on to receive her Bachelor's and Master's Degrees in Physical Education from EKU. After college, she served as women's softball coach, coed cheerleading coach, and dance team coach at Transylvania University in Lexington, Kentucky. Stephens returned to EKU to teach physical education pedagogy for K–12 before becoming the women's golf coach. She has done graduate studies on golf injuries and the analysis of the golf swing, and consulting work to produce golf feasibility studies for several Kentucky cities. She and her husband own and operate a local golf shop.

Pat and Joni currently reside in Richmond, Kentucky, and have three sons, Daniel, Ben, and Joseph.

Skills, Drills & Strategies for

Golf

Preliminaries

History of the Game

Golf, a challenging and fascinating game, is considered one of the most ancient of the modern sports. The name "golf" is thought to be derived from the Germanic term *kolbe,* or the Dutch term *kolf,* meaning club. The origin of the game is uncertain. Various games are thought to have some relationship to present-day golf, but it was the Scots who conceived the game of an individual player hitting a ball cross-country with a variety of clubs to a hole in the ground, without interference by an opponent.

As early as 1400, golf was being played in Scotland. The game became so popular during the fifteenth century that the Scottish parliament declared it illegal. Scotland was at war with England, and golf was distracting the military from archery practice. In February of 1502, a peace treaty between the warring countries was signed, followed six months later by a marital union between the King of Scotland and the daughter of the King of England. It was this union that made it possible for the Scots to return to their national diversion, the game of golf.

The traditional Scottish courses of these early years were sandy stretches of land covered by short grasses that linked the seashore with more fertile lands inland—thus the term "links." There were no tees, fairways, or greens, and hazards were numerous. Rules were few and were set up to meet local conditions. There was no set number of holes to be played. A round of golf consisted of one or more turns around whatever number of holes the course might have. Courses varied with the number of holes, some having as few as five, others as many as twenty-five. Eighteen holes eventually became accepted as the standard number of holes for a round of golf.

Early-day golf equipment differed greatly from that used in the present-day game. The ball, known as a "featherie," was made from bull's hide and feathers, and seldom stayed round. The clubs were made primarily of wood, with the exceptions of a sand iron and a utility iron for hitting balls out of ruts, and were much longer than today's clubs.

The earliest reference to golf in the United States is in 1659, in Fort Orange, New York. Not until the mid-1800s, though, did the game begin to attract attention. The first golf club in the United States was established in 1888, by John G. Reid, a transplanted Scotsman. He and his friends constructed a six-hole course in a cow pasture in Yonkers, New York, and named it St. Andrews. The site of St. Andrews changed several times, eventually moving to Mt. Hope, New York in 1892, where it became an eighteen-hole course that remains to this day.

The popularity of golf began to grow in the years between 1890 and 1900. Two years after the establishment of St. Andrews at Mt. Hope, the **United States Golf Association (USGA)** was founded out of a need for a governing body to set up rules and conduct amateur and open championships. By 1900 there were more than a thousand golf courses in the United States.

United States Golf
Association (USGA)

Golf Today

The game of golf is more popular now than it has ever been. More than 26 million people presently play the game, and each year that number grows. There are many reasons for golf's popularity. Although golf was once considered a game for the wealthy and elite, it is now a game for the general public. People of varied economic and social backgrounds can and do participate today. Access to golf courses, golf equipment, and golf instruction is at an all-time high. Some of the most popular courses in the United States are public courses.

Golf is also an activity that can be enjoyed for a lifetime. Entire families can participate, from the very young to the very old. Unlike many other sports, aging golfers do not appear to experience a great loss in skill and can continue to receive great satisfaction from participation. Golf is a game for players of all skill levels, from the beginning golfer to the golf professional. It can be played for recreation, social interaction, exercise, or sport. Competition can be intrinsic or extrinsic, as players strive to better themselves, the courses they play on, or the golfers they compete against.

Whatever the reason for participating, golf is a game that challenges and entertains those who play. The excitement of driving a ball over 200 yards, the thrill of sinking a 20-foot putt, or the satisfaction derived from one or two well-placed approach shots is enough to bring a player back again and again.

The Future of Golf

The game of golf has a bright future. Great strides have been made in many areas. Equipment has improved drastically, while staying within USGA specifications, and the increasing number of manufacturers competing in today's market ensures an even better quality of equipment in the future. Media coverage of professional golf tournaments continues to focus worldwide attention on the sport. Junior golf programs are being implemented at golf courses throughout the United States in an ever increasing number. According to the National Golf Foundation, in the year 2000 there will be 40 million golfers in the United States.

As golf continues to grow in popularity, more courses are becoming available to novice golfers. Golf courses are being built at a tremendous rate, with a great percentage of the new golf courses being public or daily-fee courses. As more people take up the game, golf instruction will reach a new high. The PGA and LPGA of America continue to train and certify golf professionals to meet popular demand. Good golf instructors will continue to get better as the curriculum becomes more uniform as a result of advanced study and research.

The following is a list of golf organizations in the United States, along with their addresses.

United States Golf Association (USGA)
Liberty Corner Road
PO Box 708
Far Hills, NJ 07931

Professional Golfers' Association of America (PGA)
100 Avenue of the Champions
Box 109601
Palm Beach Gardens, FL 33410–9601

Ladies' Professional Golfers' Association (LPGA)
300 Champions Drive
Daytona Beach, FL 32114

National Golf Foundation (NGF)
1150 South U.S. Highway One
Suite 401
Jupiter, FL 33477

The following are the major golf publications covering the sport. The first six are devoted to golf exclusively. The *Journal of Physical Education, Recreation and Dance* and *Sports Illustrated* have sections covering golf.

Golf Digest
Golf for Women
Golf Journal (published by the USGA)
Golf Magazine
Golf World
PGA Magazine
Journal of Physical Education, Recreation and Dance
Sports Illustrated

A student once remarked to her instructor at the end of a lesson, "My husband wanted me to take up an activity that didn't require any athletic skills, so we decided on golf." Unfortunately, this is an attitude that many people share. Although golf can be a relaxing social activity, it is also a sport that requires many physical skills, such as balance, coordination, strength, flexibility, and endurance. Repetitively swinging a club and striking a small white ball takes balance and coordination, as well as muscular endurance. Being able to walk, carry or pull a set of clubs, and play 18 to 36 holes takes stamina. If a golfer doesn't have muscular and cardiovascular endurance, the body will begin to fatigue toward the end of the round, affecting the golf swing.

When training for events, competing golfers can play as many as 36 holes a day, and they usually don't have the luxury of riding in a golf cart. Walking a regulation golf course is comparable to walking four to six miles. A walk of this distance would be physically tiring for many of us, especially when the course is hilly. Strength and flexibility are also necessary to play well. Shoulder, abdomen, and back strength are needed to get adequate distance on a golf shot, and flexibility allows the golfer to attain the proper positions needed in a fundamentally sound golf swing. Good upper-body strength and flexibility permit an easier, more fluid golf swing, which in turn helps the golfer play better. Physical conditioning will enable you to improve not only your golf swing but your overall physical fitness as well.

Flexibility

A year-round stretching program is extremely important for the golfer. Men usually need more flexibility work than strength work, whereas women need more strength work. Not stretching before a workout can increase the risk of injury, as can stretching incorrectly. Before stretching, warm the body up by walking at a quick pace for approximately 3 to 5 minutes. While walking, swing the arms forward and back, stretch the arms up to the side and back down, then roll the shoulders forward and back. This will increase muscle temperature and prepare the muscles for stretching.

When performing stretching exercises, use a **static stretch.** Ballistic, or bouncing, stretches should not be used because they have the potential to cause damage to soft muscle and joint tissue and actually inhibit the stretch by eliciting a **stretch reflex.** Stretching should not be painful. The stretch position will be slightly uncomfortable. After all, you are stretching the muscle beyond its original shape.

Pain is an indicator of excessive stress to the body. If you feel pain during a stretch, release the stretch to the point where the pain stops. If the pain does not go away, discontinue the exercise.

The duration of the stretch depends on its purpose. When stretching to warm up prior to activity, hold for 10 to 15 seconds. When stretching to increase flexibility after activity, hold for 15 to 30 seconds. Exhale as you move into the stretch, then breathe slowly and rhythmically while holding the stretch, in through the nose, out through the mouth. Proper breathing is important throughout all phases of conditioning.

static stretch a slow, sustained stretch to the point where the body feels a resistive tension, followed by several seconds of relaxation while holding the stretch

stretch reflex an involuntary muscle contraction in response to sudden, potentially harmful extension of the muscle

Flexibility Exercises

■ Chest stretch

Clasp hands behind your back and concentrate on pulling the shoulder blades together, stretching the chest muscles.

■ Upper back stretch

Standing with feet shoulder-width apart and knees slightly bent, clasp hands in front of chest and press palms forward. A slightly different stretch can be done by grabbing both shoulders and hugging the chest. During both of these stretches, concentrate on moving the shoulder blades away from each other.

■ Shoulder stretches

Standing with feet shoulder-width apart and knees slightly bent, cross one arm in front of your body. With the other hand, pull the arm as close to the body as possible, keeping it at chest level. Make sure the shoulder you are stretching is relaxed downward, not scrunched up toward the ear. Repeat on the other side. Another stretch can be done by placing palms with fingertips up on a wall above shoulder height. Press the head and shoulders toward the floor, bending the knees slightly to protect the lower back.

■ **Forearm stretch**

Place palms with wrists up on the wall at shoulder height. Keeping the body straight, bend the knees until you feel a stretch in the forearm.

■ **Triceps stretch**

Maintaining the same standing position as in the shoulder stretch, raise one arm above the head. With the other hand, grasp the arm below the elbow and hold it in a fixed position against the side of the head. Bend the raised arm, keeping the elbow still, and reach as far down the middle of the back as possible. Repeat on the other side.

■ **Side stretch**

Standing with feet slightly wider than shoulder-width apart and toes turned outward for balance, raise one arm above the head and stretch toward the opposite side by bending from the waist. Concentrate on keeping the waist still. Do not push the hips to one side or the other, or let them turn toward either side. Place the other hand on the thigh for support. Repeat on the other side.

■ **Hip stretch**

Standing with feet shoulder-width apart with your back to a wall, twist the torso and place palms flat on the wall at chest height. Hold. Repeat on the other side.

■ **Hamstring stretch**

Place the feet in a stride stance (one foot in front of the body, parallel to the other foot). Bending the supporting leg, keep the front leg straight and place your hands on the opposite thigh. To feel a greater stretch, lift the toe of the straight leg. Repeat on the other side.

■ **Calf stretch**

Maintaining the same beginning position as in the hamstring stretch, lunge forward onto the bent front leg. Make sure the knee on the front leg is directly over the ankle of the front leg, the back leg is straight with the toes pointed forward, not sideways, and both heels are on the floor. To stretch the deeper calf muscle, move the back leg an inch or two toward the front leg. Bend the back leg while keeping the heel on the floor. Repeat on the other side.

■ **Iliopsoas stretch**

Maintaining the same lunge as in the calf stretch, roll the pelvis forward (think about tightening the buttocks and pushing the part of the body forward where the back leg meets the front of the torso). Do not let the hip of the back leg rotate outward; keep both hips square to the front. The back leg should bend slightly as the back heel lifts from the floor. Repeat on the other side.

■ **Quadriceps stretch**

In a standing position, lift the right foot behind the buttocks, concentrating on keeping the knee close to the opposite knee and the heel lifted toward the ceiling. Holding the right ankle with the right hand, try to bring the right foot back down to the floor as though to straighten the right leg. Keep good body alignment; do not arch the lower back or let the knees move away from each other. Be sure to support yourself by placing the other hand against the wall, a table, or the back of a chair. Repeat on the other side.

■ Gluteal stretch

Lying on your back with knees bent, place the ankle of the right leg on the thigh of the left leg. Grasping behind the left thigh with both hands, pull the leg toward the chest. Make sure the right knee is pointing to the side as much as possible. Repeat on the other side. *Note:* If you feel pain in the knee joint, do not do this exercise. Instead, sit on the floor with legs together, straight in front of you, and arms straight down beside you, palms on the floor beside the hips. Cross the right leg over the left, placing the right foot on the floor beside the outer left knee, right knee pointing toward the ceiling. Sitting up straight, place the left elbow on the right knee, resting the left forearm on the side of the right leg. Turning the torso toward the right hip, use the left elbow to pull the right knee toward the left shoulder. Keep the upper body tall and lifted, the head looking back over the right shoulder. Repeat on the other side.

As stated earlier, stretching is important before beginning an activity. Prior to taking that first swing, you should do exercises to loosen up the shoulders, back, hips, and legs. Begin with the stretching exercises just described, using the golf cart for support instead of a wall (the gluteal stretch can be done in a sitting position in the golf cart), followed by these:

■ Vertebral roll exercise

Standing with feet shoulder-width apart and arms straight, hold a club in your hands so it is resting against the front of the thighs. Concentrate on the position of the vertebral column of your back. Begin to roll the body forward by slowly dropping the chin to the chest. Pretend the head, arms, and club are very heavy; let them lead the movement. Continue rolling forward as you *slowly* move the club down the legs toward the ground. Visualize each vertebra of the spine, beginning at the neck, releasing out of line one at a time as the club gets closer to the ground. Let the knees bend slightly, if necessary, to get the club completely on the ground. Hold this position for ten seconds, then reverse the process. Begin to move each vertebra back into line, starting with the lower back and proceeding upward. Again, concentrate on the heaviness of the head, arms, and club; let the re-alignment of the vertebral column pull the club up the legs. Repeat the entire exercise.

■ Rotation exercise

Beginning with the feet together, hold the club across your back and slowly twist from side to side. Keep your eyes focused on a point directly in front of the face and try to get the shoulders to alternate pointing to the front and to the back. After 8 to 10 repetitions, move the feet to shoulder-width position, and repeat. Concentrate on feeling the weight shift as you rotate. Maintaining this standing position, bend slightly forward at the waist and relax the knees. Focus the eyes on a point on the ground where the golf ball would be, and repeat the rotation exercise. Try to get the shoulders to turn 90 degrees, so the shaft of the club is pointing at your focal point. This exercise will prepare the trunk rotators for the golf swing. (See Figure 1.1.)

Figure 1.1
Rotation exercise.

a   b   c

■ **Swing exercise**

Holding two or three clubs, swing as you normally do. The added weight will help loosen the shoulders. Be sure to swing away from other golfers, to prevent possible injury to those around you. (See Figure 1.2.)

When stretching to warm up before participating in activity, remember to hold the stretch for 10 to 15 seconds. Although these warm-up stretches will take only approximately 4 or 5 minutes, they can make a real difference in your game. It is difficult to achieve a smooth, accurate shot when the muscles are tight.

Weight Training

Golfers can use weight training to increase muscular strength and endurance. Because swinging a golf club involves the hands, arms, back, abdomen, and legs and is primarily a rotary action, strength exercises should be geared toward those areas. The following exercises are recommended for use in a golf weight-training program, and serve to strengthen the parts of the body that are most involved in the golf swing.

Exercises that include the use of free weights are indicated by (FW); those using weight machines are indicated by (M). A few exercises, such as Curl-ups and Back Extension, do not require the use of weights. Off-season, pre-season, and in-season programs for the competitive golfer follow the exercise descriptions. Each program lists the exercise, number of **sets,** and number of **repetitions,** or reps, per set. The amount of weight or resistance to be used for each exercise depends on the individual. To adequately challenge the muscle, use a weight or resistance that is sufficient to fatigue the muscle by the end of the last repetition of each exercise. For example, if you are doing a set of 10 reps of the Rear Lat Pull exercise, the weight should be enough to tire the muscle to the point that you cannot perform an eleventh repetition. Keep movement slow and steady as you lift the weight *and* as you lower it to the starting position. If the exercises are too strenuous, reduce the number of repetitions or the amount of resistance/weight you are using.

sets *a group of repetitions*

repetitions *number of times the exercise is performed*

Figure 1.2
Swing exercise.

Back Exercises

■ Rear lat pull (M)

Hold lat bar with a wide grip (hands about 3 feet apart). Kneel down far enough to support the weight with the arms extended overhead. Pull bar down until it touches the back of the neck just above the shoulders, exhaling through the mouth. Slowly return the bar to the starting position, inhaling through the nose.

■ Back extension

Lie face down on a high bench while extending the upper body over the end (the hips should be at the end of the bench). Lock the legs under the bench for support, then bend down at the waist so the upper body is vertical to the floor. With hands behind the head, raise the torso up until slightly past parallel, exhaling through the mouth. *Do not arch the back.* Return to the starting position, inhaling through the nose.

Shoulder Exercises

■ **Seated lateral raise (FW)**

Sitting at the end of the bench with feet on the floor, hold dumbbells with palms facing inward, arms straight down at sides. Raise arms to the side in a semicircular motion slightly above shoulder height, exhaling as you lift. Pause, then return to starting position. This exercise can also be done standing.

■ **Thumbs-down lateral raise (FW)**

Standing with feet shoulder-width apart and holding dumbbells in hands, position your arms straight down in front of you with thumbs pointing down toward the floor. Raise your arms in a plane about 30 degrees forward, stopping just below shoulder level. Slowly lower your arms to the starting position. Exhale while raising the arms; inhale while lowering them.

■ **Rotator cuff exercises (FW)**

a. Lie on your side on a bench or on the floor. Holding a light weight in your upper hand, position your elbow close against your side with the forearm crossing the abdomen. The weight should touch the bench or floor in front of you, with your palm facing downward. Slowly raise the weight until it is pointed straight at the ceiling, exhaling as you lift. Return to the starting position, inhaling as you slowly lower the weight.

b. Turn over onto your back with your elbow tucked into your side, forearm at a 90° angle to the body. Your palm should be facing up, with the weight touching the bench or floor. Raise your weight up until it is pointing at the ceiling, keeping the elbow close to your side. Slowly return to the starting position. Exhale as you lift, inhale as you lower. Repeat entire exercise with the other arm.

Exercises for Triceps, Biceps, and Forearms

■ **Triceps curl (FW)**

Standing with feet shoulder-width apart, hold a weight in one hand and extend it overhead. Use the opposite arm to hold the upper arm close to the head. Lower the weight behind the head until the forearm touches the biceps, inhaling as you lower it. Return the arm to a straightened position above the head, exhaling as you lift the weight. Repeat with the other arm.

■ **Triceps press-down (M)**

Standing with feet shoulder-width apart, hold bar with palms down, hands about 8 inches apart. Bend the arms so forearms and biceps are touching, upper arms are close to the body. Press the bar down until arms are straight, exhaling as you press. Inhale as you slowly return the bar to starting position.

■ **Biceps curl (M or FW)**

Starting with feet shoulder-width apart, hold the bar with arms extended downward, palms forward. Exhale as you curl the bar upward toward the shoulders while pressing the elbows against your sides. Do not swing the weight or arch the back while lifting. Slowly return to starting position, inhaling as you lower the bar.

■ **Wrist curls (FW)**

a. Sitting on the end of a bench with feet apart, hold a barbell with both hands. Hands should be about 16 inches apart, palms up. Lean forward, placing forearms on the thighs, back of wrists over knees. Lower the bar as far as possible, inhaling as you lower. Exhale as you curl the bar.

b. This exercise should also be done with the palms down to work the other side of the forearms.

Exercises for Abdomen

■ Curl-ups

Lying on your back with bent knees, place your hands behind the head. The hands should not be supporting the head; only the fingertips should be touching. Exhale as you press the stomach into the floor and lift the upper body off the floor so the shoulder blades are no longer touching the floor. Slowly return to starting position, inhaling as you move down. *This should be a smooth, controlled movement.* Do not jerk up or bounce. Repeat this exercise with the legs rolled to each side to work the side abdominals, or obliques.

■ Seated side bend (FW)

Sit at the end of a bench, feet firmly on the floor. Holding the bar on your shoulders, bend to the side as far as possible, keeping both shoulders square to the front. Make sure you bend only at the waist; do not let your hips move to the side. Slowly return to starting position. Repeat on the other side, remembering to exhale as you bend down and inhale as you straighten up.

■ Seated twist (FW)

Begin in the same position as the seated side bend. Twist your shoulders to one side, keeping the head and hips square to the front and exhaling as you turn. Inhale as you return to starting position. Repeat on the other side.

Exercises for Hips

■ Hip roll

Lying on your back, place the arms straight out to each side, palms down. Bend the knees, keeping feet firmly on floor. Lower your legs to one side until the thigh touches the floor, keeping both shoulder blades on the floor. Return to starting position. Repeat on the other side, remembering to exhale as you lower the legs, inhale as you return to starting position.

■ Leg crossover

Lying on your back with arms out to each side, extend the legs straight down. Raise one leg so the toes are pointing to the ceiling, then slowly lower the leg across the opposite leg until it is as close to the floor as possible. The active leg should be at waist height or above, and both shoulder blades should be touching the floor. Return to starting position. Exhale as you lower the leg, and inhale as you lift. Repeat on the other side.

Exercises for Buttocks, Thighs, and Calves

■ Step-ups (FW)

Standing in front of a bench, place the barbell on your shoulders. Exhale as you step up with the right leg, then the left leg. Inhale as you step down with the right leg, then the left leg. Repeat, starting with left leg.

■ **Hamstring curls (M)**

Lying face down on a bench, press the back of the ankles against the padded bars. Bending at the knees, curl the bar as close to the buttocks as possible, exhaling as you curl. Inhale as you slowly lower the bar to the starting position.

■ **Knee bends (FW)**

Standing with feet slightly wider than shoulder-width and toes turned out, place a bar across the shoulders. Bend the knees as though you were going to sit in a chair, until the knees are in line with the toes, exhaling as you lower the bar. Do not let the knees get in front of or to the side of the toes. *Do not arch the back.* Squeeze the buttocks as you return to the starting position. Remember to inhale as you straighten the legs.

■ **Heel lifts (FW)**

Standing with your toes on a 2-inch block and feet slightly apart, place bar across the shoulders. Keeping the knees straight, raise up high on the toes. *Do not arch the back.* Lower the heels until they touch the floor. Exhale as you lift, and inhale as you lower the bar. This exercise can also be done with toes pointed in or out.

Off-Season Program

During the off-season, the goal of the weight-training program should be to strengthen the major muscle groups and provide necessary muscle balance. Workouts should be done 3 days per week, with a day of rest between each workout. Include some cardiovascular exercise (discussed next), such as jogging or swimming, in your program.

EXERCISES	SETS	REPS
Leg crossover	1	10 to 20 each side
Curl-ups	1	15 to 25 knees to ceiling
		15 to 25 knees to right side
		15 to 25 knees to left side
Seated twist (optional)	1	10 to 20 each side
Seated side bend	1	10 to 15 each side
Wrist curls	1–2	10 to 15 per set
Rear lat pull	2	10 per set
Back extension	1–2	8 to 15 per set
Rotator cuff exercises	2	10 per set
Triceps press-down	2	10 per set
Knee bends	1	15 to 30 per set
Step-ups	1–2	10 to 15 per set each leg
Heel lifts	1–2	10 to 20 per set

Pre-Season Program

During the pre-season, the weight-training program should consist of exercises that continue to strengthen the major muscle groups plus work on various body parts. Workouts should be done 2 days per week, with 1 to 2 days rest between workouts. Cardiovascular exercises, such as incline walking on a treadmill, should be included in your program.

EXERCISES	SETS	REPS
Hip roll	1	15 to 25 each side
Curl-ups	2	20 to 30 knees to ceiling
		20 to 30 knees to left side
		20 to 30 knees to right side
Rotator cuff exercises	3	10 per set
Triceps curl	2	10 to 15 each side
Seated side bend	2	10 to 15 each side
Seated twist (optional)	1	15 to 25 each side
Wrist curls	1–2	15 to 20 per set
Step-ups	2–3	10 to 15 per set each leg
Back extension	2	8 to 15 per set
Hamstring curls	2–3	10 to 15 per set

In-Season Program

When in-season, your goal should be to maintain levels of muscular strength and endurance you have achieved. Work on hip, forearm, and wrist strength is optional. Workouts should be done 2 days per week, with 1 to 2 days rest between workouts. Be sure to include cardiovascular exercises throughout your training program.

EXERCISES	SETS	REPS
Curl-ups	2	20 to 30 knees to ceiling
		20 to 30 knees to left side
		20 to 30 knees to right side
Back extension	1–2	8 to 15 per set
Rotator cuff exercises	2–3	10 per set
Seated side bend	1–2	10 to 15 each side
Seated twist	1	15 to 25 each side
Knee bends	1	25 to 50
Triceps curl	2	10 to 15 each side
Rear lat pull	2	10 per set

Proper breathing technique is important during weight training. Breathe in through the nose and out through the mouth. Exhale during the exertion, or work phase, of the exercise. Be sure to warm up and stretch prior to performing any strength exercises, and always stretch at the end of the workout.

Aerobic Conditioning

To prevent the body from fatiguing during a round of golf, some type of cardiovascular or **aerobic exercise** should be done regularly. Jogging, swimming, biking, circuit training, and aerobic dance are all excellent aerobic activities. Also, many types of aerobic equipment can be bought for use in the home, such as exercise bikes and treadmills. For golfers who are just beginning to work on cardiovascular endurance, walking is one of the safest and simplest exercises. A vigorous walk increases the heart and respiratory rate sufficiently, while placing less stress on the lower extremities than some other forms of aerobic exercise. Whichever activity you choose, you should participate at least three times a week for 20 to 60 minutes to achieve a fitness benefit.

aerobic exercise rhythmical large-muscle activity of moderate intensity performed for at least 20 minutes without interruption

EQUIPMENT

Basic pieces of equipment used in the game of golf include a set of clubs (woods, irons, putter), a golf bag, golf balls, tees, a golf glove, and golf shoes. A seemingly unlimited variety of equipment is available to the beginning golfer. Bags, clubs, balls, gloves—how does the beginner know which to choose?

Clubs

Before investing money in the finest, most expensive clubs, consult with a golf professional. He or she can suggest an inexpensive set with which to begin. A full set of golf clubs is not necessary. A driver, 3-wood, 3-, 5-, 7-, and 9-irons, and a putter will suffice as a starter set. Woods are shaped differently than irons (see Figure 1.3) and are not necessarily made of wood. In fact, most woods today are made of metal. The woods provide greater distance than the irons, and the driver, or 1-wood, delivers more distance than the other woods.

A full set of irons includes the long irons (#1, #2, #3, #4), middle irons (#5, #6, #7), and short irons (#8, #9, pitching wedge). A sand wedge, a lob wedge, and a putter are considered specialty clubs. Each club has a distinctive **loft.** The loft of each club increases as the number of the club increases (see Figure 1.4), whether it is a wood or an iron.

loft the degree the clubface angles from the vertical plane

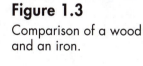

Figure 1.3
Comparison of a wood and an iron.

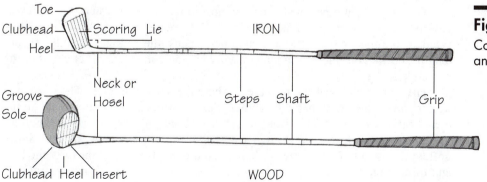

Figure 1.4
Club loft.

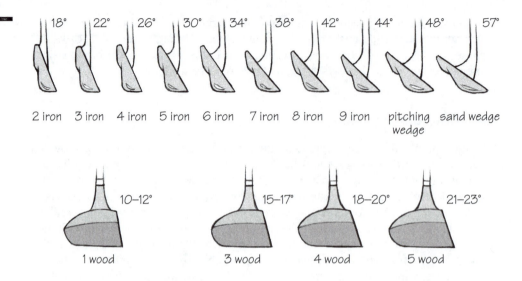

trajectory the path of
the ball through the air

swingweight the total
weight of the club multi-
plied by the distance from
a specified point from the
grip end—12 or 14 inches,
depending on the scale—
to the point at which the
golf club balances

putter club used to roll
the ball into the hole on
the green

offset putter a putter
whose putting blade is
behind the shaft of the
putter

The greater the loft, the higher is the **trajectory** of the ball. As skill develops, the need to invest in a complete upgraded set of clubs becomes more evident. Often a golf professional will allow you to trade in a beginner's set for a complete-ly matched set of your choice. A complete set of clubs usually includes a driver, a couple of other woods, 3-, 4-, 5-, 6-, 7-, 8-, and 9-irons, pitching wedge, sand wedge, and putter. For competitive play, the maximum number of clubs allowed in your bag during a round of golf is fourteen.

When selecting clubs, the length, swingweight, and shaft flexibility should be considered. The length of a club can affect the distance of a shot. The longer the club, the greater is the clubhead speed and the greater the distance you can hit the ball. For beginning golfers, using clubs with greater length than a standard set often results in less accuracy. Therefore, highly skilled golfers will use longer clubs more effectively than beginning golfers. A traditional standard set of men's irons starts at 35 inches for the pitching wedge and increases in length by a half inch up to 39 inches for a 2-iron. Women's clubs usually are a half inch to an inch shorter than men's.

Swingweight and total weight are important factors in the general feel and playability of the club. Changing the swingweight of a club can affect a golfer's shotmaking ability considerably, as can shaft flexibility. The golf professional will recommend the appropriate swingweight for you, dependent on the club length and shaft flexibility.

The types of shafts include steel, aluminum, graphite, and titanium. Shaft flex-ibility and weight vary among styles. The latest trend is to use a lighter shaft and a heavier clubhead. This may not be right for every individual, though. Trust your local golf professional to help you make the right choice.

The **putter** could be considered the most important club you own, when you consider the fact that par on most courses is 72, and 36 of those strokes are allo-cated to putting. When choosing a putter, check the putter for style, shape, length, and weight. These components will help the golfer feel better about his or her stroke.

There are a wide variety of putters. There is no perfect putter. The right put-ter for you is an entirely personal choice. Some golfers prefer putters with align-ment markers on top of the head to assist in lining up the putt. Some golfers prefer putters with thicker grips because they discourage wrist action. Some golfers choose an **offset putter** to help keep the hands slightly ahead of the ball and discourage wrist action. The heavier feel of a mallet head putter might be the putter of choice for golfers who need to slow down their putting stroke.

Some people find one putter they like and use it throughout their golfing experience. Others may change putters on a regular basis, searching for that elusive "perfect" putter.

Golf Bag

Unlike the early pioneers of golf, today's golfers prefer to carry their clubs in a golf bag. The golfer's ability level and amount of play should be a factor when picking out the right golf bag. Small golf bags are needed if you prefer walking when playing. Medium-size bags are a good choice if you intermittently walk and ride when playing. Large golf bags are a good selection if you need a bag that travels better and holds more equipment.

Golf Balls

Traditionally, the golf ball is white, although golf balls now come in a variety of colors. Trying to purchase the proper golf ball can be difficult if one does not know a little about the characteristics of the golf ball. The make-up of the ball is important in choosing the correct one.

Golf balls fall into two basic categories, two-piece and three-piece. The two-piece ball is simply a cover over a synthetic core inside. The three-piece ball consists of a small solid or liquid-filled rubber core, rubber thread wound around the core, and a cover. The covers can be made from several different materials, the most popular being the **Surlyn®** used primarily on two-piece balls, and a synthetic **balata.**

Any golf ball covered with Surlyn® is durable and will not cut as easily as a balata type. The durable cover is needed by beginners, and golfers looking for more roll. The balata cover, found mainly in a three-piece ball, is a softer cover that cuts easily. It is recommended for experienced golfers with better playing ability. In general, Surlyn®-covered two-piece balls bounce higher on hard surfaces and slice or hook less than the three-piece balata ball, whereas the balata ball spins more readily and has a higher trajectory than the two-piece Surlyn®.

The **compression** rate is usually considered when purchasing a golf ball. The difference in compression from 80 to 100 does not make a significant difference in the distance the ball travels; however, there is a difference in the feel of the ball. Stronger hitters prefer the 100-compression ball because it feels harder than the 80- or 90-compression balls.

Surlyn® hard, cut-resistant material made by the DuPont Company

balata synthetic form of the dried green-like juice from a West Indian tree

compression relative hardness of the golf ball

Tees

Tees are small pegs used to elevate the ball from the ground on the first shot of each hole. They are made from wood or plastic and come in various colors and lengths. They can be used with any club the golfer chooses to hit from the teeing ground. The driver, or 1-wood, is most commonly used when teeing the ball. Because the driver does not have as much loft as other clubs, the ball should always be teed up when hitting with it.

Place the tee in the ground so the height of the ball to the driver is half the ball above the clubface (see Figure 1.5). When using an iron, tee the ball about a half inch above the ground for a long iron, a quarter inch for a short iron. Using a tee instead of placing the ball on the turf gives the golfer the best possible opportunity to make solid contact with the ball. Beginners should keep a plentiful supply of tees in their bag in case of breakage during tee shots.

tee wooden or plastic peg on which the ball is placed

Figure 1.5
Clubface to height of ball.

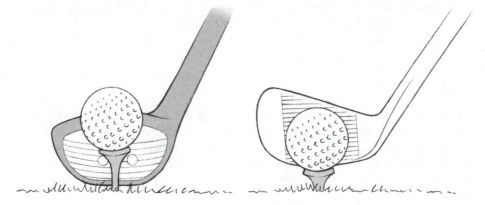

Glove

A glove is an integral part of the golfer's equipment. The glove helps prevent the club from slipping or twisting in the hand on impact. Right-handed golfers wear a glove on their left hand; left-handed golfers wear one on their right hand. Wearing a glove on the non-dominant, or target, hand establishes a feeling of grip security. Leaving the dominant hand gloveless provides a better sense of feel when swinging the club. It is not recommended that golfers wear gloves on both hands, unless necessary during inclement weather.

Shoes

Walking 18 holes can be hard on the feet, so shoes should be comfortable and durable. Many beginning golfers wear some type of athletic shoe, rather than purchase a special pair of golf shoes. Athletic shoes are acceptable but do not provide as secure a stance as spiked golf shoes, especially when hitting a ball from an uneven lie or damp ground. Most experienced golfers wear some type of spiked golf shoe to assure a firm, balanced stance during play. For golfers who wish to play in golf shoes but who do not like the hard spikes, many of today's golf shoes are made with soft spikes. The new soft spikes are thought to cause less wear and tear on greens and still provide enough traction to prevent slippage.

The Game/ The Activity

The foundation of a good golf game is a sound golf swing. The golf swing is a rotary motion controlled by the large muscles of the body, primarily the legs, hips, back, trunk, shoulders, and arms. The swing is a fluid motion of controlled energy, an almost effortless chain of events resulting in a dynamic release of power. The full swing is used throughout a round of golf, with modifications in the short game when chipping, pitching, and putting.

Chipping and pitching are referred to as **approach shots.** Good approach shots can make up for an inadequate shot or can place you in a position to make an easy putt. Developing and refining these skills can improve your score considerably. Putting, thought by some to be a game within a game, is an important skill in golf. Putting uses special skills and knowledge different from those needed for the rest of the game, yet seems to be one of the least practiced golf skills. This is surprising, considering that good putting skills can result in significantly lower scores. Other essential skills include sand play, rough play, and uneven lies.

Golf is generally regarded as an individual sport, a game that pits the golfer against the golf course. This idea attracts a lot of people, particularly those who prefer to participate in a sport that does not require a playing partner or a group. Golf can be played with partners or teams, too. Scramble, best ball, alternate shot, and other team events can be enjoyable. For those interested in participating in such events, local golf courses generally have men's, ladies', and junior leagues that play team games. Whichever one chooses—individual, partner, group, or team—golf is still a game of humans against nature, the golfer against the golf course.

approach shot stroke made with the intent of having the ball finish on the green

RULES AND VIOLATIONS

The game of golf has many rules. As a beginner or novice, however, it is not necessary to know the entire *USGA Rules Book.* Listed below are some basic rules that are important for golfers to know when learning to play. For a complete list of rules and regulations, keep a rule book in your golf bag for a quick reference during play.

1. The purpose of the game is to make as few strokes as possible during the course of a round of golf.

2. The golf ball is played from the position where it is found unless changed through local rules.

3. Golfers must play from each hole's respective teeing area. The ball must not be teed in front of the tee marker and no more than two club lengths behind the tee markers.

honors *the privilege of hitting first*

4. The golfer who has the lowest score on the previous hole has the **honors** on the next tee.

5. When playing a golf hole, the golfer who is the farthest away always hits first.

mark *to place a small object, preferably a coin or plastic marker, behind the golf ball*

6. Golfers may **mark** the ball when on the putting green.

7. Golfers are not permitted to touch the line of a putt unless they are repairing a ball mark or old cup mark. Spike marks made by golf shoes that are in the line of the putt cannot be tapped down before putting.

8. When the golfer is in water or sand hazards, the golf club cannot touch the water or sand during the address or the backswing. The golf club may touch the hazard during the downswing.

stroke-and-distance penalty *penalty stroke given when the ball is lost, hit out-of-bounds, or hit in a water hazard, and the player puts another ball into play from where the ball was last hit*

9. Golf balls that are hit out-of-bounds must be replayed from the point where the shot was last played and a penalty stroke added to the score. This is referred to as a **stroke-and-distance penalty.** If you hit the ball out-of-bounds from the tee box, you would be hitting your third stroke from the tee box. You may hit a **provisional ball** if you think your ball has gone out-of-bounds. If the first ball *is* out-of-bounds, the provisional ball would then be played to finish the hole. If the first ball is in-bounds, the provisional ball is picked up and the hole is played with the original ball.

provisional ball *a second ball hit from the original position of a ball that is thought to be out-of-bounds or lost*

10. When a ball is lost, you are allowed a maximum of 5 minutes to look for it. If you are unable to find the ball within that time limit, go back to where you hit the ball and hit another ball, adding one penalty stroke (stroke-and-distance penalty). If you hit a ball that you think may be lost, you may hit a provisional ball. This saves you the time of having to walk back to the place the ball was last hit and hitting again, which would slow down play. If you are unable to find your original ball after 5 minutes, the provisional ball would then be played to finish the hole.

11. When a golf ball is hit into a water hazard marked by yellow stakes or lines, you: (a) play the ball as it lies, (b) take stroke-and-distance penalty, or (c) drop behind the hazard on a line between the point where the ball last crossed the margin of the water hazard and the hole and take one penalty stroke.

12. When a golf ball is hit into a lateral water hazard marked by red stakes or lines, options include: (a) playing the ball as it lies, (b) taking stroke-and-distance penalty, (c) dropping behind the hazard on a line extending from the hole through the point where the ball last crossed the margin of the water hazard and taking one penalty stroke, (d) dropping within two club-lengths of the point where the ball entered the hazard no closer to the hole and taking one penalty stroke, or (e) dropping on the opposite side of the hazard at a point the same distance from the hole as the point of entry, adding one penalty stroke. You are not allowed to play a provisional ball for a ball hit in a water hazard or lateral water hazard.

13. A golfer who has a ball with an unplayable lie can: (a) drop within two club-lengths of the unplayable lie and no closer to the hole with a one-stroke penalty, (b) drop behind the ball, with no limit to distance, along a line extending

from the hole through the spot where the ball was unplayable, adding one penalty stroke, or (c) play from the spot where the ball was last played with a stroke-and-distance penalty.

14. When an immovable obstruction interferes with the intended swing or stance, the golfer may drop within one club-length of the nearest point of relief that avoids interfering with the swing or stance without a penalty stroke, as long as the point is no closer to the hole and is not in a hazard or on the putting green.

PLAYING AREA

A golf course usually has 18 holes, although there are some 9-hole and 36-hole courses. A round of golf is 18 holes. When playing on a 9-hole course, the golfer plays the course twice, but from different teeing areas. An 18-hole course is usually par 70, 71, or 72, measuring anywhere from 6,000 to 7,200 yards, with a mixture of par 3's, 4's, and 5's. Most par-72 courses will have four par 3's, ten par 4's, and four par 5's.

Although each hole is uniquely different, there are common elements. A golf hole has one or more **teeing grounds** (designated starting place for each hole), a **fairway** (closely mowed playing area between the tee and the green), **rough** (the grassy area skirting the fairway that is less manicured than the fairway), **boundaries** (outer perimeter beyond which play is not allowed), **fringe** (grass surrounding the green that is shorter than the fairway but longer than the green), and a **green** (closely mowed area of golf course that contains the hole, cup, and flagstick). Most holes also have hazards, such as **sand bunkers** (hazard filled with sand within the boundaries of the golf course), or **water hazards** (water obstacle defined by red or yellow stakes/lines), positioned in strategic places along the fairway or around the green to handicap inaccurate players. Figure 2.1 provides an illustration of a typical golf hole, showing these features.

teeing grounds
fairway
rough
boundaries
fringe
green
sand bunkers
water hazards

SCORING

The object of the game of golf is to get the ball into the hole using as few strokes as possible. There are two methods of scoring in golf: **stroke play** and **match play.** Stroke play, sometimes referred to as medal play, is more commonly used than match play. When using this method, players record the number of strokes per hole, then add up their total score for the round. The winner is the player with the lowest score. In match play, the golfer tries to win each hole by having the fewest strokes. If both players have the same number of strokes on a hole, they halve the hole and no one wins that hole. The player who has won more holes at the end of the round is the winner. The match can be over before the end of the round if a player is up by one more hole than the number of holes left to play.

Scores are recorded on a scorecard (see Figure 2.2). The card indicates the yardage and **par** for each hole, as well as the difficulty of the hole in relation to **handicap.** It also has a place to record scores for each hole and an area for attesting to the accuracy of the score.

Par is determined by the yardage and difficulty of the hole. Holes having shorter distances of up to 249 yards for men and 210 yards for women from tee to green are normally delegated as par 3's. Holes with distances of 250 to 470 yards for men and 211 to 400 yards for women are par 4's. The longest holes are the par 5's, with distances of 471 yards and longer for men and 401 to 575 yards for women. Some courses even have par 6's for women when holes are longer than 575 yards. Some commonly used scoring terms include **hole-in-one** (ball is hit into the hole from the teeing ground in one stroke), **double eagle** (three strokes under par), **eagle** (two strokes under par), **birdie** (one stroke under par),

stroke play a competition between golfers determined by who completes the round with the fewest strokes

match play a competition between golfers determined by who wins the most holes

par number of strokes that an expert golfer is expected to make for a given hole

handicap the average number of strokes a player's score is over par

hole-in-one
double eagle
eagle
birdie

Figure 2.1
Illustration of a golf hole.

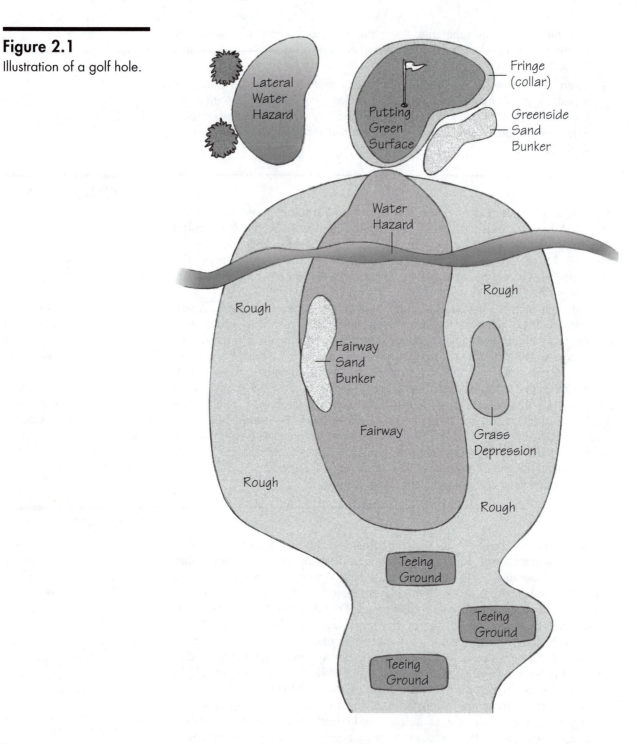

bogey
double bogey
triple bogey
holes up
all square

bogey (one stroke over par), **double bogey** (two strokes over par), **triple bogey** (three strokes over par), **holes up** (having won more holes than your competition during match play), and **all square** (having won an equal number of holes as your competition during match play).

ETIQUETTE   While playing the game of golf, each golfer should observe the proper behavior on the golf course. By following the proper golf course etiquette, the game will be more enjoyable for everyone.

		1	2	3	4	5	6	7	8	9	OUT
BLUE	70.2/119	369	388	493	460	214	395	162	443	397	3321
WHITE	68.9/116	349	359	493	456	182	364	162	428	377	3170
PAR		4	4	5	5	3	4	3	4	4	36
HANDICAP		15	9	3	13	11	5	17	1	7	OUT
HOLE NUMBER		**1**	**2**	**3**	**4**	**5**	**6**	**7**	**8**	**9**	**OUT**
	+/-/0										
HANDICAP		15	9	3	13	11	5	17	1	7	**OUT**
PAR		4	4	5	4	3	4	3	4/5	4	35/36
RED	70.2/119	292	336	409	330	162	271	162	329/426	331	2622/2721

All yardage from tees, sprinkler heads, and 150 yard markers are measured to the center of green.

PLEASE - Replace Divots
Rake Sand
Repair Ball Marks   Scorer_____   Attest_____   Date_____

Figure 2.6
Sample scorecard.

1. Safety is an important consideration when playing golf. Golfers should never walk behind or in front of other golfers when they are hitting.

2. The golfer who has the honor should always play first from the teeing area. Some courses, however, encourage doing away with honors and hitting when ready, to speed up play. After teeing off, the golfer farthest away from the hole should play first.

3. The golfer should be prepared to hit when it is his or her turn. When fellow golfers are hitting, other golfers should be still and quiet to prevent disrupting concentration. No talking or practice swinging!

4. Golfers should never hit until the group of golfers in front are completely out of range. At the same time, it is important to try to keep pace with the group in front of you so as not to slow down play.

5. If a group is playing slowly, it should let faster groups play through. A round of golf should be completed in 4 hours or less.

6. The golfer should watch hit balls carefully so they will be easier to find. When looking for lost balls, golfers should not take too much time. Spending too much time hunting for a lost ball slows play for all the groups following your group. Maximum time limit is 5 minutes.

7. When hitting, the golfer should warn other golfers of an approaching ball by yelling "Fore!"

8. The golfer should recognize fellow players' good shots and overlook bad ones.

9. When on the green, the golfer shouldn't step on another player's **line.**

10. Golfers should not drag their feet when walking on the green. Spiked shoes can leave damaging marks. All spike marks should be repaired before leaving the green.

11. The golfer should repair all **ball marks** with a divot tool, rake sand bunkers after use, and replace **divots** created when hitting the golf ball. Golfers should try to leave each hole in better shape than when they arrived to play.

line the direction the ball will take when putted

ball marks small indentations on the putting surface made by a ball hit into the green

divots pieces of sod cut by a clubhead during a swing

12. The person whose ball is closest to the hole should attend the flagstick. He or she should not drop the flag on the green but, rather, should lay it down carefully out of the way of each golfer's extended putting line. The first person to complete the hole should be ready to replace the flag upon the group's completion of the hole.

13. Upon completion of a golf hole, golfers should immediately proceed to the next tee box before marking scores.

14. Golfers should familiarize themselves with local course rules and abide by them.

Skills and Drills

The golf swing is a fluid motion that requires coordination of the large and small muscles of the body. Most golfers are searching for that elusive "perfect" swing. They want to look like a PGA touring professional, hitting one effortless, errorless shot after another. But not all golfers are the same height and weight. Not all have the same degree of strength, coordination, and flexibility. Because of this, each individual will look different swinging the golf club. There is no such thing as a perfect swing that fits everyone. There is, however, a best swing for every golfer, composed of basic swing fundamentals that assist the golfer in making a sound, fluid golf swing.

SKILL 1 The Full Swing

Pre-swing fundamentals include the grip, set-up, alignment, and pre-shot routine. In-swing fundamentals include the takeaway, backswing, downswing, and followthrough. Deviations in the fundamentals will influence either the path of the swing or the position of the clubface on impact. The relationship between the swing path and clubface position will determine the direction of the ball flight (see Figure 3.1). A straight ball flight will always result when the angle between the clubface and the swing path at the moment of impact is a 90-degree angle. When the angle is less than or greater than 90 degrees, the ball will follow a curved path. The beginning golfer's objective is to develop a swing technique that works with his or her individual physical attributes to produce a consistent ball flight, one that can be duplicated again and again, that will enable him or her to land the ball in the desired spot.

Pre-Swing Fundamentals

Grip

The grip is the most taught fundamental of the golf swing. The proper grip position allows the hands to act as a unit. There are a variety of golf grips, and golfers should choose the one with which they feel most comfortable. The following grip

Figure 3.1

Relationship of clubface position to swing path to ball flight (illustrated for a right-handed golfer).

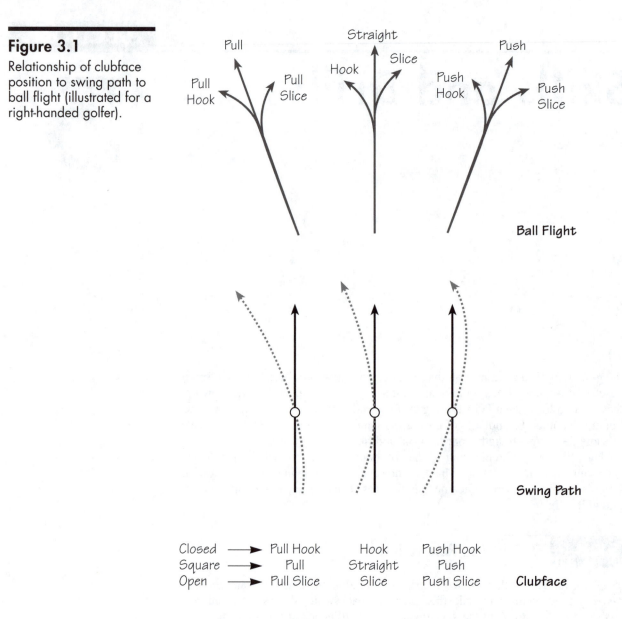

Closed	→	Pull Hook	Hook	Push Hook	
Square	→	Pull	Straight	Push	
Open	→	Pull Slice	Slice	Push Slice	**Clubface**

positions are described for right-handed and left-handed players. The term "target hand" refers to the hand that is closest to the target and grasps the handle first when setting the grip (left hand for right-handed golfers, right hand for left-handed golfers). "Back hand" refers to the hand that is farthest away from the target and grasps the handle last when setting the grip.

The **Vardon overlapping grip** is achieved by placing the club in the palm and fingers of the target hand as illustrated in Figure 3.2. Close the hand around the club, pointing the thumb down the shaft. Place the middle two fingers of the back hand under the club, with the third finger touching the target hand. Close the back hand around the club, making sure the lifeline of the back hand overlies the thumb of the target hand. The thumb of the back hand will point slightly to the target side of the shaft.

The **interlock position** is accomplished as described for the Vardon grip, except the last finger of the back hand is actually placed between the first and second fingers of the target hand instead of overlapping the first finger of the target hand. Players who prefer this grip position think it provides them with a stronger, more secure grip because the hands are forced to move as a single unit.

Vardon overlapping grip grip position in which the last finger of the back hand overlaps the first finger of the target hand

interlock position grip position in which the last finger of the back hand interlocks the first finger of the target hand

The **ten-finger position,** or baseball grip, is the most popular among beginning golfers. All ten fingers are contacting the club, in much the way that a baseball player holds a bat. This provides the golfer with a greater feeling of control over the club. The disadvantage of this grip position is that the hands have a tendency to act as separate parts, making it more difficult to maintain a stable unit.

Whichever grip position you choose, remember to keep the palms facing each other, and try to keep the back of the target hand square to the target. Improper placement of the hands can result in a variety of shot problems, such as a **hook** or **slice.** A simple cue to achieve proper palm position is "target-back, back-middle," often referred to as "left-right, right-middle" for right-handed golfers, and "right-left, left-middle" for left-handed golfers (see Figure 3.3). When gripping the club, the thumb and first finger of each hand forms a "V." The "V" of the target hand should point to your back shoulder, while the "V" of the back hand should point to the mid-point between your back shoulder and chin.

Grip pressure is just as important as grip position. Grip pressure should be firm, not tight, and evenly distributed throughout the grip. Many novice or beginning golfers tend to apply pressure by pushing thumbs down on grip, and often develop blisters after swinging many times with this grip pressure problem. Some golfers assume a death grip on the club. If pressure is too great, the entire golf swing becomes tight and inhibited, making a fluid swing difficult to achieve. In contrast, if grip pressure is too light, the club will move in the hand, preventing the golfer from contacting the ball with a square club face. The golfer should try to concentrate on having strong fingers and flexible wrists, and on keeping the arms and shoulders relaxed and light.

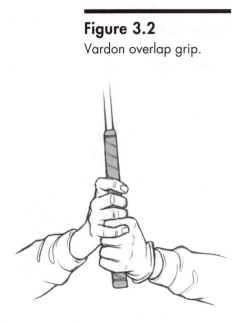

Figure 3.2
Vardon overlap grip.

ten-finger position grip position in which all fingers on both hands wrap around the club

hook golf shot that curves from right to left for right-handers and left to right for left-handers

slice golf shot that curves from left to right for right-handers and right to left for left-handers

"V"s are formed by the thumb and forefinger of each hand.

Figure 3.3
Target-back, back-middle.

Figure 3.4

Hand position
under the club.

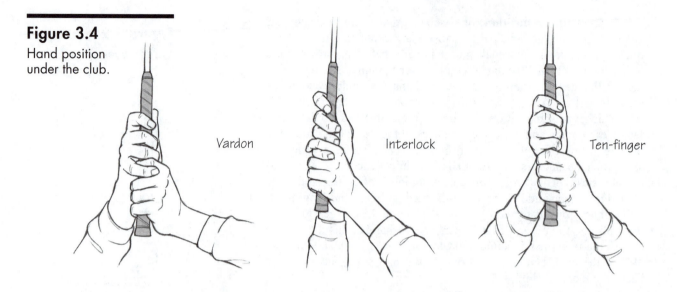

Vardon · Interlock · Ten-finger

When working on grip position and pressure, the student golfer should hold the club in front of the body. Placing the club on the ground is not necessary. Holding the club straight out or even pointed toward the sky allows the grip to be more readily seen. Although the hand position on the top of the club is what the golfer sees, the position on the underside will define the grip position (see Figure 3.4).

The key to any good grip is that it enables the student golfer to make a swing that will return the clubface to the square position at impact. The golf grip is the only connection the golfer has to the golf club. Therefore, that connection must be comfortable and easily replicated so the position can be reproduced every time the swing is to be made. When the golfer has to fight to get the proper position and pressure of the grip, the swing will often be affected in a negative way. Table 3.1 lists some grip errors and how to correct them.

Grip Checklist

- pressure firm and even
- strong fingers, flexible wrists
- arms and shoulders relaxed
- V's "target-back, back-middle"
- hands form a stable unit

TABLE 3.1 Possible Grip Errors and Corrections

ERROR	RESULT	CORRECTION
Grip too tight	Inhibited release of club	Even pressure with both hands
Grip too light	Loss of control of clubface	Even pressure with both hands
Palm of back hand too far under shaft	Hook or pull	Replace palm facing target
Palm of back hand too far over shaft	Slice	Replace palm facing target
Back of target hand too far under shaft	Slice	Replace target hand so back of hand faces target
Back of target hand too far over shaft	Hook or pull	Replace target hand so back of hand faces target

Set-Up

A good set-up position should feel balanced and natural. Stand with the insteps of your feet shoulder-width apart, and assume an athletic posture. Your weight should be balanced, centered toward the balls of the feet, the knees slightly flexed. Bend over just enough to let your arms hang straight down from your shoulders and away from the body. You should not feel as though you are leaning forward or reaching for the ball. If you feel as though you are going to lose your balance or you must use your club to keep your balance, you may have too much weight distributed toward the toes or the heels, or you are not using the shoulders and hips for counterbalance. As you assume your grip and place the club on the ground, notice the position of the back shoulder. The back shoulder will be slightly lower than the target shoulder, because the back hand is placed farther down the club than the target hand. The hands and grip should be positioned slightly inside the front thigh and approximately 4 to 6 inches from the body, as shown in Figure 3.5.

Proper ball position is critical to hitting a good golf shot. Over the years, golf instructors have taught two different methods for attaining correct ball position. Some instructors believe that the ball position stays constant in the **stance.** The ball is played off the target heel in the stance, with the back foot changing position depending on the club. The main advantage to this method is its simplicity—it is easily replicated.

The other technique is a variable ball position (see Figure 3.6). The ball position works its way back in the stance as the club gets shorter. To find the correct

stance *position of the feet when the player addresses the ball with all golf clubs*

Arms hang almost vertical from shoulders.

Keep weight balanced on both sides of this line.

Figure 3.5
Athletic posture
(set-up position).

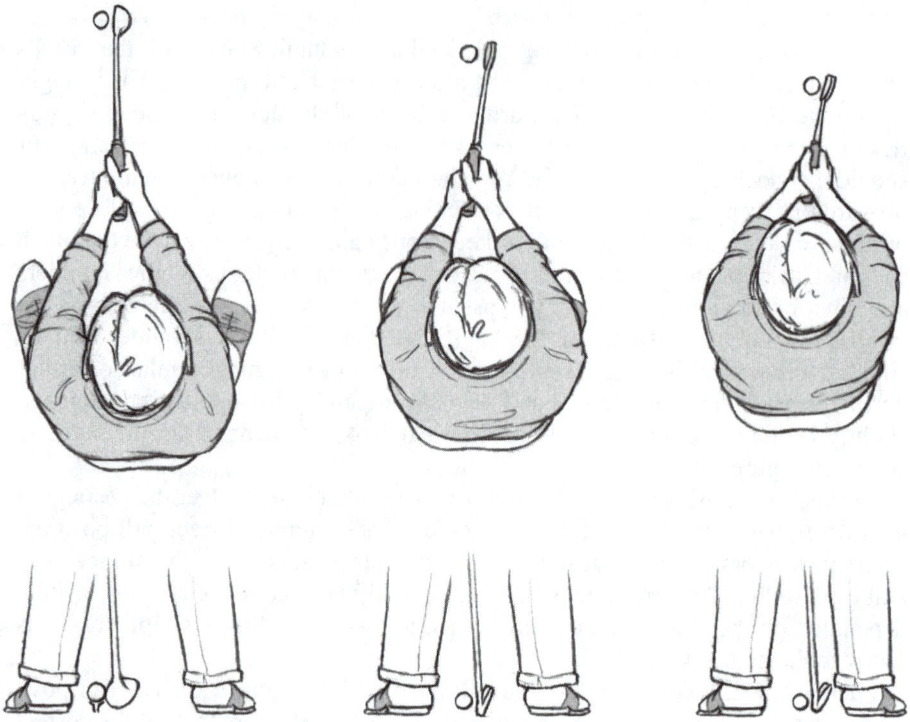

Figure 3.6

Variable ball positions.

ball position with this method, each individual must practice placing the ball at various positions until he or she develops a feel for what works best. Whichever technique you use, the goal is to find the position of the golf ball where the club-face meets the ball at the correct angle and moment during the swing that produces a good shot toward the intended target. Table 3.2 lists some set-up errors and how to correct them.

TABLE 3.2   Possible Set-Up Errors and Corrections

ERROR	RESULT	CORRECTION
Standing too close to the ball	Fade or slice Shank	Reposition stance; perform *On Again, Off Again* and *Mirror Check* drills
Standing too far away from the ball	Topping the ball Push or pull	Reposition stance; perform *On Again, Off Again* and *Mirror Check* drills
Ball too far back in stance	Pop-up	Reposition stance; perform *Two Step* drill
Ball too far forward in stance	Hitting fat Hitting thin	Reposition stance; perform *Two Step* drill
Ball too far back in stance and club chopping down at ball too steeply	Deep divots, low shot	Reposition stance and focus on one-piece takeaway; perform *Two Step* drill and *Keeping the Triangle* drill

Set-Up Checklist

- feet shoulder-width apart between insteps
- athletic posture (knees slightly flexed, upper torso bent at waist)
- weight evenly distributed along feet
- arms hanging freely from shoulders
- back shoulder slightly lower than front shoulder
- hands/grip positioned inside front thigh 4 to 6 inches from body

Alignment

Being able to line up to the target is a crucial element of the pre-swing fundamentals. If you are unable to correctly align yourself with the target, you will not get the desired result, no matter how good your swing. Some people literally try to aim their feet and body to the target. This is a misconception. You want to aim the *clubface* at the target, then position your feet, hips, and shoulders along a line that is parallel to the target line (see Figure 3.7). Beginning golfers should concentrate primarily on the clubface and feet alignment. As they become more familiar with their golf swing, they can work on shoulder and hip alignment. Some people find it difficult to ascertain whether they have correct alignment, particularly when the target is a long distance away. To remedy that, find a spot on the ground about 3 or 4 feet in front of you on your target line. Align your clubface with the spot, and your feet, hips, and shoulders parallel to the spot, and you'll be right on line. Table 3.3 lists some alignment errors and how to correct them.

Figure 3.7

Correct alignment of body and club.

TABLE 3.3	Possible Alignment Errors and Corrections	
ERROR	**RESULT**	**CORRECTION**
Aiming to right of target (RH) or left of target (LH)	Slice or shank Hitting fat	Adjust alignment; perform *Correct Alignment* drill

Alignment Checklist

- clubface square to target
- feet aligned parallel to target line
- shoulders and hips aligned parallel to target line

Drills for Pre-Swing Fundamentals

Grip

Drill #1: Club Up for Grip

Hold club in target hand. Position club directly in front of you with clubhead pointing to the sky. Check grip position; notice where the V's formed by the first finger and thumb on each hand are pointing (target-back, back-middle). Place club on the ground, making sure clubface is square to target and V's of hands are still properly aligned. Repeat five times or more, until you are able to properly grip the club consistently.

Drill #2: Grip Pressure

Establish your grip on the club. Point clubhead to the sky with your grip directly in front of you. Squeeze the grip as tightly as possible. Feel the tension in your hands, arms, and shoulders. Hold for 5 seconds, then gradually loosen the grip to the point where the club is almost sliding through your hands. When the club begins to slide, grip the club just tightly enough to stop the club from slipping, stressing the firmness of the last three fingers of the target hand. This is the proper grip pressure. Repeat this drill at least 10 times.

CUE: pressure firm, not tight

Set-Up

Drill #3: Athletic Position

Standing with feet shoulder-width apart, grip the club, keeping the clubhead pointing at the sky. Holding the hands still and firm, flex the knees and lean slightly forward from the waist, slowly lowering the arms until the clubhead is on the ground. Your body should be in a balanced position, with weight evenly distributed along the feet. This is the natural club position for your set-up. Repeat this drill at least 15 times.

CUE: flex and lean, lower the arms

Drill #4: On Again, Off Again

First, choose a partner for this drill. Then, using a middle iron, place the clubhead on the ground as though setting up to a ball. Have your partner hold the shaft so you can release the club without it falling or moving. Let your arms hang naturally from the shoulders, then swing them onto the club, assuming your grip. Release and repeat this action until you can consistently acquire a correct, comfortable grip and arm position.

CUE: grip, release; grip, release

Drill #5: Two Step

With the feet together, stand to the side of the ball. The ball should be even with the target foot. After aligning the clubface, move your target foot toward the target and your back foot away from the target. The distance you move the feet will depend on the length of the club. For short irons, the ball should be slightly forward of center; with long irons, the ball should be closer to the heel of the target foot. The longer the club, the more you move your back foot to widen your stance.

Drill #6: Mirror Check

Standing in front of a full-length mirror, set up as though addressing the ball, keeping your shoulders parallel to the mirror. Mentally check the following elements:

- muscles in the arms, chest, and shoulders are relaxed, not visibly tense or bulging
- grip pressure on the club is firm, not too tight, not too light
- insides of the feet are shoulder-width apart
- hand position is slightly ahead of the ball

Now change your address position so you are hitting the shot at the mirror. Check to see that:

- knees are slightly bent and weight is toward the balls of the feet
- clubface is square to the target/mirror
- feet, hips, and shoulders are parallel to your target line
- the grip end of the club is approximately 4 to 6 inches away from your body

Alignment

Drill #7: Correct Alignment 1

After setting up to the ball, lay one club on the outside of the ball pointing directly at the target. Lay another club in front of your feet parallel to the first club. Lay a third club just inside your target heel at a 90-degree angle to the other clubs. Practice hitting balls, checking to make sure that clubface is square to the target, feet and hips are parallel to the first two clubs on the address, and front foot is just in front of the third club. (See Figure 3.8.)

CUE: clubface square to target, feet and hips parallel to target line

Drill #8: Correct Alignment 2

Once you feel comfortable with your feet and hip alignment, try this drill. Lay a club on the ground outside the ball pointing to your intended target, and another club in front of your feet pointing down a line parallel to your target line. Ad-

Figure 3.8
Correct alignment 1.

dress the ball, then place a club across your chest, noting where the club is pointing. Turn your head to look at the target; be careful not to raise up or let the body turn as you look. The club should be pointing down a line parallel to your target line. Hit the ball, observing the path of the ball in relation to the target. If the feet, hips, and shoulders are properly aligned, the shot should go straight. If it does not, the missed shot is probably caused by some other factor, such as grip or swing path.

CUE: shoulders parallel to target line

Figure 3.9
Spot check.

Drill #9: Spot Check

Place headcovers at three or four different spots on the line between your ball and the target. Choose one of the headcovers for your intermediate target. Try to hit the ball directly over the headcover. Note where the ball lands. Continue hitting balls, using a different headcover as your intermediate target each time until you find the one that consistently gives you the best end result. (See Figure 3.9.)

Pre-Shot Routine

Before a golfer strikes a golf ball, an established routine is needed to consistently get into a proper set-up. You should use this routine every time you set up to hit a ball. Following the same routine every time gets you into a rhythm and helps clear your mind of distractions, focusing your attention on the shot at hand. We recommend that you always start your pre-shot routine from behind the ball. Here you can survey the terrain and visualize the shot you want to make. Then go through your routine, addressing the ball and aligning yourself and the club to the target. The following is a suggested routine that many golfers use. You may choose to follow this routine as is, make modifications, or develop your own routine.

1. Starting from behind the ball, analyze the hole, and visualize the shot.
2. Take your grip and practice swing from behind the ball.
3. Spot check (find a spot on the target line about 3 to 4 feet away), then walk to the ball.
4. Stand with feet together, ball even with target foot.
5. Set clubface to point at spot on target line.
6. Move the target foot forward the distance needed to get proper ball position, then step back with back foot so feet are shoulder-width apart.
7. Check to see if line of feet is parallel to target line.

You are ready to hit.

In-Swing Fundamentals

In-swing fundamentals include the takeaway, backswing, downswing, and followthrough. Drills are presented so you can practice these.

Takeaway

The first motion in the golf swing is done by swinging the club back. This movement combines the action of the hands, arms, clubhead, shoulders, chest, and hips moving away from the ball as a one-piece unit (see Figure 3.10), keeping the clubhead as low to the ground as possible. The one-piece takeaway gets the golf swing going in the correct sequence. The triangle formed by the arms and chest at address should stay intact during the takeaway. The rest of the body remains relatively still. Because the golf swing is a rotary motion, the hips will begin to turn as you feel the urge to turn. Table 3.4 lists some takeaway errors and how to correct them.

Takeaway Checklist

- one-piece takeaway
- club low to ground
- triangle intact

Backswing

Once you do the takeaway correctly, the muscles along the side of the torso will start to stretch. As the muscles stretch and the hip turn begins, there is a change in weight distribution. No longer is the weight evenly dispersed between both feet; the weight begins to shift toward the back foot. Halfway through the backswing, the golfer should be in the position noted in Figure 3.11. The toe of the golf club will be pointing up with the thumbs up on the grip. The butt of the grip of the club should be in line with the top of the toes and pointing down the target line. This is a fundamentally sound position. As you can see from Figure 3.11, the hands or wrist have yet to set (or cock).

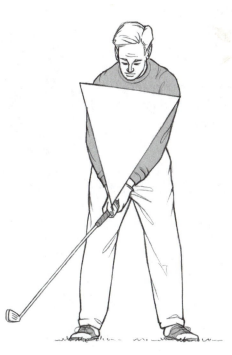

Figure 3.10
One-piece takeaway.

1) Practice

2) Slow Backswing

3) Pong-Pong Us Tennis
   Driver vs. Wedge

4) Lady Golfers

5) Turn vs. Sway

6) Open vs. Close

7) Tee Drill / P.39

8) P.33

TABLE 3.4	Possible Takeaway Errors and Corrections		
ERROR		**RESULT**	**CORRECTION**
Lifting or picking up the club		Slice or pull	Low, extended takeaway; maintain triangle
Fanning the clubface (turning target hand over the club so palm is facing body, clubface is open)		Inconsistent shot patterns	Keep back of hand facing target

Backswing Checklist

- full shoulder and hip rotation
- weight shift toward back leg
- gradual hand set to top
- target shoulder under chin
- back facing target
- club parallel to ground

Completion of the backswing is a continuation of the rotation or turn of the shoulders and hips, with the weight shift toward the back foot, the front shoulder under the chin, and the gradual set of the hands at the top of the backswing. To get the energy you want to hit the ball a great distance, this coiling of the body is imperative.

Most beginning golfers have too much wasted motion. Their bodies move in unnecessary paths, the most common being a back-to-front swaying motion. To prevent backward swaying during this rotation, point your target knee toward your back knee and rotate your hips until your back faces the target.

The ability to get a full turn with your back facing the target will result in a powerful backswing. The top of the swing, however, may appear different from individual to individual. Some golfers are able to get the golf club to a higher position on the backswing because of more flexibility. The golfer should take the golf club back only as far as the body will allow. The desired position is one in which the club is parallel to the ground, as shown in Figure 3.12. Once the backswing is complete, the golfer will be ready to start the downswing. Table 3.5 lists some backswing errors and how to correct them.

Figure 3.11 (on left)
Backswing.

Figure 3.12 (on right)
Top of backswing.

TABLE 3.5 Possible Backswing Errors and Corrections

ERROR	RESULT	CORRECTION
Backward swaying motion of body	Inconsistent shot pattern; no power	Emphasize still head, full hip and shoulder turn; target knee points to back knee, as right hip rotates to the back
		Use the *Keeping Head Centered* drill or the *Stop Swaying* drill
Upward body movement	Whiffed or fat shot	Emphasize keeping head still, maintaining athletic posture
No shoulder turn, swinging with arms only	Slice or pull	Stress back facing target at top of backswing, target shoulder under chin
Club dropping below horizontal at top of backswing, because of:		
Loose grip	Slice or pull	Check grip pressure; perform *Grip Pressure* drill
Bent target arm	Whiffed or fat shot	Emphasize maintaining target arm extension and full hip and shoulder rotation; use *Backward Sweep* drill
Open clubface	Slice	Check grip, set-up, alignment; correct wrist position at top
Closed clubface	Hook or pull	Check grip, set-up, alignment; correct wrist position at top

kinetic chain
casting

Downswing

The downswing is started from the ground up. The energy transfer begins with the feet, legs, and hips, followed by the shoulders, then extends through the arms, hands, and club. This is known as the **kinetic chain,** an energy-creating sequence of movements that are each a result of preceding actions. This motion is made in most ball sports, including baseball, softball, tennis, and racquetball. The weight transfer from the back leg to the front leg and the rotation of the hips are made first to get the slower, larger muscles out ahead (see Figure 3.13). The power of the swing begins with this movement, not the swing with the arms.

Casting, or starting the downswing with the arms, is a common mistake in beginning golfers and can result in missed shots. Remember that the arms should naturally follow the hips. The faster the hips rotate during the downswing, the faster the arms and hands will work, pulling the body around to a finished position.

What most beginning golfers don't realize is that *swinging* smoothly produces more clubhead speed than *hitting* hard. Trying to hit the ball hard often interrupts the pendulum action of the swing, turning it from smooth to erratic. The rate of rotation during the downswing should

Figure 3.13
Beginning of downswing.

Key here is
the speed
of hip turn

Figure 3.14

Impact position.

be a smooth tempo or speed, not slow, then fast, or fast, then slow, but rather a building of momentum as the swing gives in to gravity.

Hitting a golf ball far and with control is a result of good rhythm and timing. A swing starts slowly and builds up speed until it is at maximum speed at the bottom of the arc. As the body uncoils, the hands and wrists follow with the golf club on the way down through the impact area. The swing's maximum energy is released when the target arm and the club form a straight line on impact and the centrifugal force of the clubhead passes through and strikes the golf ball. (See Figure 3.14.) Table 3.6 lists some downswing errors and how to correct them.

Downswing Checklist

- weight shift from back leg to target leg
- hips uncoil
- arms and hands follow hips
- smooth swing
- straight line from target arm through club on impact

Followthrough

The followthrough occurs after the clubface impacts the ball. Although the followthrough does not have any direct effect on the shot, a correct followthrough is indicative of a fundamentally sound swing. If the upper body and hips have been coiled and uncoiled properly during the swing, the body will have been "unwound" into a correct finish position. Picturing the followthrough position (see Figure 3.15) also gives the mind something to focus on other than impact.

Many beginning golfers have a tendency to stop the swing when the club makes contact with the ball, causing the club to decelerate as it approaches the ball. Deceleration on the downswing is going to result in reduced power and an opening of the club face, giving the golfer less than desirable shot outcomes. If the golfer strives to end the swing in the proper finished position, he or she will be

TABLE 3.6	Possible Downswing Errors and Corrections	
ERROR	**RESULT**	**CORRECTION**
Casting with hands or arms	Slice or pull Weak or fat shot	Focus on lower body weight shift toward target and letting wrists uncock naturally; use *Partner Pull* or *Step Swing* drill
Hands behind clubhead at impact	High shot Topped shot	Focus on lower body weight shift toward target and letting wrists uncock naturally; use *Partner Pull* or *Step Swing* drill
Forward swaying motion of body	Push Low shot	Focus on keeping head still; emphasize correct leg action, hip and shoulder rotation; use *Keeping Head Centered* drill

No holding back as right arm rolls over left.

Figure 3.15 (on left)
Followthrough.

Figure 3.16 (on right)
Finished position.

more likely to hit *through* the ball, instead of at it, achieving the necessary acceleration at impact to produce a solid, powerful hit.

The finished position should be a relaxed, balanced position. The golfer's weight should be on the front foot, with the torso facing the intended target. The knee of the back leg should be pointing to the target, and the weight remaining on the back foot should be on the toes. Hands should be high over the front shoulder, the clubhead pointing toward the ground behind you. (See Figure 3.16.) Table 3.7 delineates the most common followthrough error and how to correct it.

Followthrough Checklist

- weight on target foot
- back knee facing target
- torso square to target
- hands high over target shoulder
- clubhead pointing to ground behind you

TABLE 3.7	Possible Followthrough Errors and Corrections	
ERROR	**RESULT**	**CORRECTION**
Lack of extension into high finish	Slice, loss of distance	Emphasize finishing with hands high; use *Brush Away* drill

Drills for In-Swing Fundamentals

Drill #10: Keeping the Triangle

Using your driver, set up as though to a ball, noting the triangle formed by your arms and chest. Grasp your driver just below the grip on the steel or graphite part of the shaft. The grip should be pointed at your stomach. Swing the club halfway back and halfway through, working on keeping the grip pointed at your stomach and keeping the triangle formed by the arms and chest throughout the swing. Good trunk rotation is necessary to keep the grip in this position, as well as keeping the upper arms close to the body. Feel that one-piece takeaway, as the arms and body work together to begin the swing. (See Figure 3.17.)

Drill #11: T's Up

Address the ball, forming a triangle with your arms. Swing halfway back so the hands are at waist level and the shaft of the club is almost parallel to the ground. Stop and check the position of the hands and the clubhead. Your thumbs and the toe of the club should be pointing upward. Now swing halfway into the followthrough. Stop and check your hand and club position. Again, your thumbs and the toe of the club should be pointing upward. Regular use of this drill will result in a solid, one-piece takeaway and a square clubface on impact.

Drill #12: Keeping Head Centered

Have a partner stand in front of you. Without a club, address a "pretend" ball. When you are set, have your partner extend his or her arm and place his hand on your head, holding it securely in place. Take several "swings," trying to keep your head still while making a full hip and shoulder rotation. Repeat this drill at least 25 times, then try to hit some practice shots, concentrating on using the same motion.

CUE: head still, full rotation

Drill #13: Head on Wall Drill

Stand facing the wall. Assume your stance so your head is against the wall. Holding the grip of the club in your target hand and the shaft in your back hand, palms out, bend the elbows and bring the club in to your chest. Rotate the hips and shoulders as though taking your backswing, concentrating on keeping your head against the wall. (See Figure 3.18.)

Figure 3.17
Keeping the triangle.

Drill #14: Stop Swaying

Assume your stance. Place two extra balls under your back foot. Try to brace your back foot against the balls so that only the inside of the foot is touching the ground. Take a practice swing, concentrating on rotating the hips, keeping the weight on the inside of the back foot during the weight shift of the backswing, and not letting the body sway past the back foot. After several practice swings, hit 10 to 15 balls.

CUE: *hip rotation, brace back foot*

Drill #15: Backward Sweep

Using a 5-iron or 6-iron, set up to the ball. Place another ball about 12 inches behind and slightly inside the first ball. As you begin your takeaway and backswing, try to sweep away the second ball with the back of the clubhead as the body rotates. (See Figure 3.19.)

CUE: *smooth, deliberate takeaway; sweep the ball*

Drill #16: Target Arm Extension at Top

Perform the first part of the *T's Up* drill, stopping the club in your backswing parallel to the ground and checking the position of your

Figure 3.18
Head on wall drill.

Figure 3.19
Backward sweep.

thumbs and the toe of the club. Keeping the target arm frozen in this position, rotate the shoulders so the upper back is facing your target, as you pull the target shoulder under the chin. Hold this position for 5 seconds, then return the club to parallel position. Repeat five more times.

CUE: target arm extended throughout backswing

Drill #17: Step Swing

Address a teed ball in your normal position. Bring the target foot back so the feet are together. Start your backswing; as it reaches the top, step forward with your target foot, letting the leg action begin the downswing. Concentrate on making a smooth swing and weight shift while making solid contact with the ball. (See Figure 3.20.)

Drill #18: Partner Pull

Set up toward a target, with your partner standing a club-length behind the club, facing the target. Slowly swing the club back until the shaft is parallel to the ground. Stop the club in this position, and have your partner grab the clubhead. Attempt to perform your downswing from this point, trying to pull the clubhead out of your partner's hands. (See Figure 3.21.) Feel the hips and legs move toward the target and the back arm move close to your side, as the muscles along the target side of the torso tighten. After repeating this drill several times, have your partner change positions so that he or she can grasp the clubhead when you reach the top of your full backswing. Again, try to pull the club out of your partner's hands as you begin your downswing, concentrating on the feeling of the target side of the body *pulling* the club through the ball.

Figure 3.20
Step swing.

a

b

Figure 3.21
Partner pull.

CUE: pull with target side as weight shifts toward target, back arm close to side

Drill #19: Heel Springs

Set up to a "pretend" ball. Take your backswing, visualizing a spring under your target heel, pushing the heel off the ground. As you move into your downswing, feel the spring under your back heel driving the heel up into your finish position. Repeat this drill 10 to 15 times, then hit some balls, using the same mental image. (See Figure 3.22.)

CUE: spring up; target heel, back heel

a   b

Figure 3.22
Heel springs.

Figure 3.23

Legs start downswing.

a   b   c

Drill #20: Legs Start Downswing

Set up in your address position, holding a 5-iron or 6-iron in your front hand (hand closest to the target). Using only the front hand, slowly take a full backswing, focusing on a spot on the ground where your ball would be. Rotate the upper body so the front shoulder is under the chin at the top of the backswing. Begin the downswing by shifting your legs toward the target, letting the body pull the club and arm around. Swing through to a balanced finish, with the front elbow bending as you followthrough. Repeat this drill at least 20 times a day. (See Figure 3.23.)

CUE: slow backswing, shift legs toward target, finish

Drill #21: Tire Drill

Using an old tire and an old iron club, set up with the edge of the tire just inside your target heel. Take a normal swing, holding the position when the club contacts the tire. Note whether the target arm is in a straight line with the club, shoulders are slightly open to the target, and the back arm is close to the side. Adjust accordingly. Repeat this drill until you can repeatedly achieve the correct impact position. (See Figure 3.24.)

CUE: Freeze on impact, check position. Do not swing so hard that you hurt yourself!

Drill #22: Feet Together

With the feet close together, swing a short iron. Concentrate on the weight shift, moving the knees toward each other (target knee toward back knee on backswing, and back knee toward target knee on downswing) and rotating the hips, ending in a fin-

Figure 3.24
Tire drill.

ished, balanced position. When you become comfortable with the swing and are able to maintain your balance, try hitting several balls from this stance. Start with the ball teed, concentrating on making solid contact rather than hitting for distance. When you consistently make solid contact with the ball, try hitting balls on the turf. Gradually progress the feet out to shoulder-width apart, continuing to focus on the above-mentioned points. (See Figure 3.25.)

Figure 3.25
Feet together.

Drill #23: Pendulum Action

Set up with an iron, as though to strike a ball. Take a small swing, bringing the club back and forth about 6 inches off the ground. Concentrate on letting the natural movement of the arms, hands, and club turn the body. As the club comes forward to the desired position in each followthrough, let gravity return the club to the ground and immediately begin another backswing. Continue taking small swings, slowly increasing the size of the swings until you are making full, uninterrupted swings. Do not let your arms swing independently from the body.

CUE: clubhead back and through, arms and body work together, continuous swings, work to full swing

Drill #24: Brush Away

Place a leaf, twig, or coin approximately 12 inches in front of your ball. Hit the ball, concentrating on trying to brush away the object with your club after impact.

Drill #25: Back Hand Release

Using a 5-iron or 6-iron, set up to a teed ball with only your back hand (hand farthest away from the target) on the club. Swing slowly, using only the back hand and taking a three-quarter backswing and a smooth downswing. Be sure to coil and uncoil the body, keeping the back arm close to your side. Feel the back hand return the clubface to a square impact position, as you concentrate on making solid contact with the ball. Finish the swing in a full, balanced position.

CUE: slow three-quarter backswing, smooth downswing, solid contact, full finish

Drill #26: Slow Pitch for Full Swing

Using a sand wedge or 9-iron, hit balls over a bush or some other object about chest high and 3 yards away. Use about half of your inherent power to lob the ball over the target with a full but slow swing. Keep your grip pressure light, and swing with a smooth tempo. As you continue to perform this drill, you will begin to improve your touch, increase your coordination, and heighten your awareness of your swing.

CUE: full swing, slow smooth tempo, light grip pressure

Drill #27: Eyes Closed

After warming up, set up to a teed ball. Just as you get ready to begin your takeaway, close your eyes. Take a full swing, keeping the eyes closed until after impact. Concentrate on the body parts working in smooth sequential order, and try to make solid contact with the ball. After you hit the ball, open your eyes to monitor the direction and distance of the ball in relation to your intended target. Repeat this drill until you can routinely hit the ball solidly.

CUE: eyes closed, smooth swing, solid contact

SKILL 2 | The Short Game

The short game consists of chipping, pitching, and putting. These are explained in the following pages and drills are included for each.

A chip is designed to roll . . .

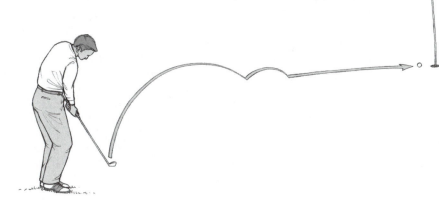

Figure 3.26
Chip shot.

Chipping

The object of a chip shot is to hit a low-flying shot that gets the ball rolling as quickly as possible (see Figure 3.26). Chip shots require a short backswing and an accelerating downswing. One of the most common mistakes in chipping is to take the club back too far and too fast for the short shot. Consequently, golfers who over-swing try to compensate by slowing down, or decelerating, during the down-swing. Consistently accurate shots become difficult to achieve when the golf club is slowing down at club impact.

To set up for the chip, open your stance by dropping your target foot back and bringing both feet closer together. This will give you a clearer view of your shot, by moving your target shoulder out of your line of vision. Shift more of your weight toward your front foot, and align the ball with the back foot so it is underneath your back ear.

Using a short iron, take a short backswing, lifting the clubhead up crisply from the ground and never taking the club higher than waist height. Accelerate through the ball, using a descending blow on the downswing and keeping the hands ahead of the clubhead.

Keep your target arm firm throughout the swing, maintaining a flat wrist until after impact. Do not try to scoop the ball. Shorten your followthrough. A chip should feel more like a hit-and-hold shot, with the club staying low to finish and an incomplete shoulder turn. Figure 3.27 illustrates how to hit a chip shot.

Chipping Checklist

- narrow, open stance; weight forward
- short, upward backswing
- descending blow on downswing
- target wrist flat
- accelerate through the ball
- club low to finish

Chipping Drills

Drill #28: Chip Swing

Assume your stance, holding a short iron in the target hand only. Swing the club approximately one-quarter the full swing, concentrating on the back of the target

Figure 3.27

Hitting a chip shot.

a

b Hands stay in front of club.

c Hold finish low.

hand, pulling the club through on the forward swing. After 10 to 12 swings, grip the club with both hands. Note the triangle formed by the arms. Swing the triangle back and through, approximately one-quarter of a full swing, letting your back elbow bend slightly on the backswing and keeping the target arm firm throughout swing. As you continue this pendulum action, shift more weight to the target foot, as though leaning toward the target. Perform 10 to 12 more swings in this position.

CUE: *one-quarter swing, target arm firm, lean toward target*

Drill #29: Upward Backswing

Address the ball. Place a second ball about 6 inches behind the ball you are going to hit. Using the arms and shoulders, chip the ball, keeping the clubhead from striking the second ball during the backswing and downswing.

Drill #30: Target Wrist Flat

Place a long comb or tongue depressor under the back of your glove. Practice your chip swing, feeling the resistance of the comb against the back of the target wrist. Continue swinging, working to prevent the wrist from bending, until you no longer notice the resistance. Try chipping a few balls, still keeping the target wrist flat so you feel no resistance from the comb.

CUE: *target wrist flat, no resistance*

Drill #31: One-Handed Chip

Set up to hit your chip shot. Holding the club with the target hand only, take the clubhead back, keeping it below waist height. On the downswing, make a slightly descending blow, letting the target hand accelerate the club through impact. Hit 10 to 15 balls. Repeat the drill until you feel like you have control on the one-handed shot, then try using both hands.

CUE: *descending blow, accelerate through the ball*

Drill #32: Landing Target

Place ten balls about 2 to 3 feet from the green. On the putting green, place a club 2 feet from the edge of the green so the shaft is parallel to the edge of the green where the balls are. Form four landing areas by placing four more clubs on the green parallel to the first club and 2 feet apart, at distances of 4, 6, 8, and 10 feet from the edge of the green. Hit each ball, trying to land between the two closest clubs on the first bounce. Continue this drill, working toward the farthest landing area. Keep a record of how many balls landed inside each area. Each time you perform this drill, try to improve your record until you can successfully land eight of ten balls in each landing area.

CUE: concentrate on landing area

Drill #33: Chipping for Distance

Place a club 8 feet from the edge of the green so the shaft is parallel to the edge of the green where you are standing. Hitting ten balls, try to chip them as close to the shaft of the club as possible without actually touching it. Note where the ball has to land to roll the correct distance. When you can get eight or more balls within 10 inches of the target, move the club back 3 feet and repeat the drill.

Pitching

The swing for the pitch shot (see Figure 3.28) is simply a larger version of the chip shot, but it is a higher-flying shot that stays longer in the air than it travels on the ground. The player assumes a slightly wider open stance to support a fuller swing. Using a pitching or sand wedge, the player takes a higher upward backswing. The downswing still requires a descending blow, accelerating through the ball, but the pitch is a hit-and-release shot, with the upper body completing a full shoulder turn during the followthrough, ending with chest facing the target and hands high. Figure 3.29 illustrates how to hit the pitch shot.

Pitching Checklist

- open stance
- high backswing
- descending downswing
- accelerate through the ball
- full finish (chest to target, hands high)

█ Pitching Drills

Drill #34: Sidearm Toss

Place a ball in your back hand, then assume your address position. Bring the ball back between waist and shoulder height, then toss the ball toward the target in a low sidearm pattern. Concentrate on turning the upper torso to face the target and finishing with the back arm extended toward the target, back hand even with the target side of the face.

Drill #35: Over Golf Bag

Place 8 to 10 golf balls in the grass beside the putting green. Place your golf bag about 3 feet in front of the

Figure 3.28
Pitch shot.

A pitch is designed to fly.

Figure 3.29
Hitting a pitch shot.

Full turn, high finish, chest faces target.

balls, between the green and the balls. Practice pitching over the golf bag, concentrating on taking a high backswing and making a descending blow. Try to get the ball over the bag without touching it. After hitting all the balls, collect them and repeat the drill.

Drill #36: Rope Drill

Tie a rope approximately 3 feet above the ground. With a short iron and 10 to 15 balls, position yourself 4 to 5 feet away from the rope. Try to *chip* the balls underneath the rope. After hitting all the balls, collect them and repeat the drill, this time trying to pitch the balls *over* the rope.

Drill #37: Up and Down for Nine

up and down finish the hole with one chip or pitch and one putt

With a partner, choose nine different locations from around the green. Try to chip or pitch onto the green and one putt. The winner is the player who can get **up and down** the most "holes."

Drill #38: Target Ball

For this drill you will need a pitching wedge or 9-iron and 12 balls. Place a ball on the ground; mark your hitting spot by placing a tee in the ground beside the ball about 6 inches away. Pitch the ball a short distance, but at least one club length. Hit a second ball from the same spot, trying to hit the first ball with the second ball either on the bounce or the fly. Score one point if hit on the bounce and 5 points if hit on the fly. The ball that is the farthest distance from your hitting spot becomes the new target ball, which you will now try to hit with a third ball. Continue trying to hit the target ball, (the ball farthest from you), using all 12 balls. As each ball is hit, the distance of the target will increase, making each consecutive shot more difficult. Keep a cumulative score. Each time you perform this drill, try to increase your score.

Putting

Putting is a skill in golf that everyone has the capacity to acquire, and good putting can be the fastest way to improve one's score. Putting does not require a lot of muscle strength or endurance. Compared to the full golf swing, putting has little movement other than the motion made by the arms and shoulders, similar to the first motion made in the one-piece takeaway. For a golfer to excel and become a good putter, he or she must follow certain key putting fundamentals, be able to read greens, and spend an abundant amount of time practicing.

How should you hold the putter? There are several acceptable styles, shown in Figure 3.30. Whichever style you choose, the putter should feel comfortable in your hands and allow a smooth putting stroke. Choose a grip style that accomplishes these things.

Figure 3.30
Styles for holding a putter.

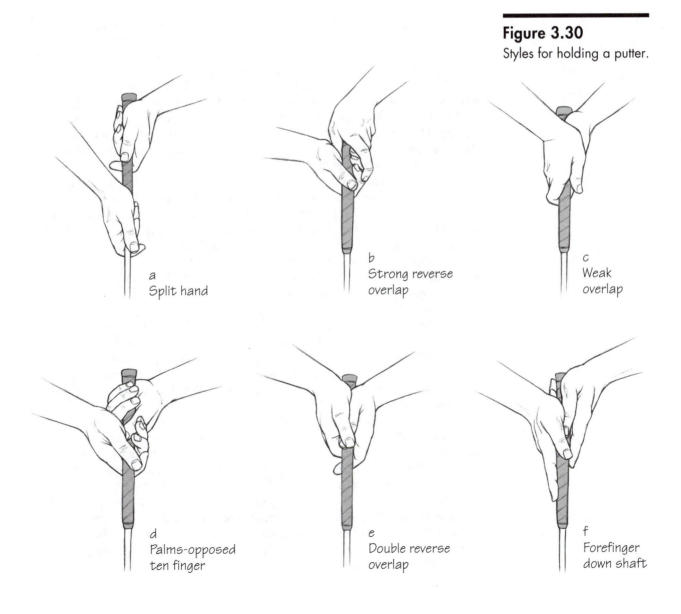

a
Split hand

b
Strong reverse
overlap

c
Weak
overlap

d
Palms-opposed
ten finger

e
Double reverse
overlap

f
Forefinger
down shaft

Figure 3.31

One unit—putter, hands, arms.

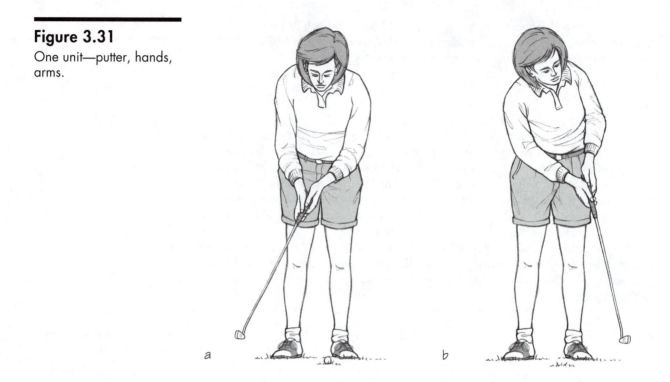

a   b

The putting stroke should be a pendulum motion. When putting, rid the body of any excess movement, keeping the head and the lower body still throughout the stroke. The putter, hands, and arms should work as one unit, with the hinge action occurring at the shoulder joint, not the wrists (see Figure 3.31). If one hand takes over during the stroke, you will lose control of the distance and direction of your putt. By using the one-piece pendulum motion, you will be better able to return the clubface back to a square position on impact and send the ball in the desired direction.

The width of your stance is not important. A golfer may have a wide, narrow, open, or closed stance, as long as the stance is comfortable and allows the body to remain balanced and steady throughout the stroke. Where the weight is distributed is not important. What is important is that the weight does not shift during the putt. Some golfers put more weight on the front foot when putting to help prevent a weight shift. Ball position in the stance should be slightly forward, with the hand position even or slightly ahead of the golf ball. Keep your eyes directly over the ball, so you have a clear and accurate view of the putting line (see Figure 3.32).

The length of the putting stroke is directly related to the length of the putt. For short putts, a short stroke is needed, whereas a longer putting stroke is necessary for putts of longer distances. The ball should be hit using a pendulum motion, with a slight acceleration on the forward stroke. The length of the backswing should match the length of the followthrough, with the putter staying close to the ground throughout the stroke.

There is more to putting than the mechanics of the stroke and proper alignment. For a golfer to be a proficient putter, he or she must be able to read the break of a putt. When beginning golfers learn to putt, they do most practice sessions on a relatively flat surface on the putting green to develop a consistent putting stroke.

When putting during a round of golf, most putts will not be straight or level. The break of a putt is influenced by a variety of elements, the most crucial being the slope of the terrain and the direction of the **grain.** The slope can be uphill, downhill, sidehill, or combinations of these. The grain of the grass can be toward the hole, away from the hole, or at angles to the hole. Grain follows water runoff, mowing cuts, sun, and prevailing wind directions.

grain *direction the blades of grass grow and lie on the green*

a   b

Figure 3.32
Eyes over ball, ball
slightly forward.

In reading a green, it is important to view the putt from various positions. First, look at the putt from behind the ball. This is the best view for determining the break of a putt. If it looks straight from this view, it probably *is* straight, and there may be no need to look at the putt from any other angles. If there is a steep hill, mound, side hill, or double break, though, a view from another perspective might be necessary. A side view can help you determine whether the putt is uphill, downhill, or across a mound, information you need to decide on the break and speed of the putt.

A look at the hole itself to inspect the grain will give you further clues as to speed and break. When putting with the grain, the ball will break more and roll farther than when putting against the grain. Looking at the grass around the rim of the hole will clearly show the grain. If you are still unclear about the putt, walk around to the other side of the hole and take a look at the putt from behind the hole. This will serve two purposes: It will give you a feel for the firmness of the green, and it will give you a view of the break around the hole. Further hints for reading a green include the following.

- The firmer the green, the faster the putt.

- A putt tends to break more going sidehill and downhill than uphill.

- Balls roll faster when traveling in the direction the grass is growing. If the grass looks dense and green from where you stand, the grass is growing toward you and you will be putting into the grain. If it looks shiny, it is growing away from you and you will be putting downgrain, or with the grain.

- Most putting greens are either bentgrass or bermuda grass. Bentgrass is a cool-season grass that, when grown and maintained properly, will have little grain. Bermuda grass is a warm-season grass that will always have grain to some degree. A good rule of thumb is: When putting on a bentgrass green, read the slope of the green. When on bermuda grass, read the slope and grain of the green.

- Because the grass grows during the day, greens usually putt faster in the morning than in the late afternoon.

- When the green is near water, the putt has a tendency to break toward the water.

Putting Checklist

- ball forward in stance
- hands even or slightly ahead of ball
- eyes directly over ball
- one-piece pendulum motion
- no weight shift
- length of backswing should match length of followthrough

Putting Drills

Drill #39: Keeping Time

Pretend your putter is the pendulum on a grandfather clock. To stroke the ball, the pendulum must go back and forward. In a slow, even, "tick, tock" rhythm, bring the putter back on the "tick," forward on the "tock."

Drill #40: Yardstick Drill

Place a yardstick on the putting surface. Position a ball beside the 18-inch mark on the ruler. Vary the distance of your backstroke, beginning with 2 inches and working up to 12 inches. From each distance, putt the ball five times, making sure your backstroke and forward stroke are equidistant each time you putt. Observe how far the ball rolls as the length of your backstroke increases.

Drill #41: Putting Swing Path

Lay two clubs on the green parallel to each other and to the line of the putt so the grip of each club is beside the hole. The distance between the clubs should be just enough to allow the head of the putter to fit between them. Place a ball between the clubs and set up for the putt. Check to see if the putterface is square to the target and at right angles to the clubs on the ground. If it is not, make the necessary adjustments. Stroke the ball, noting the path of the backswing and followthrough of the putt. The putterhead may move slightly to the inside of the club closest to your feet but not to the outside of the clubs. Continue this drill until you can consistently keep the putterhead within the clubs throughout the putt. (See Figure 3.33.)

Drill #42: Name Straight

Place a ball about 2 feet from the hole with the imprinted name pointing down the target line. Try to stroke the ball into the hole, keeping the name straight to the target as the ball rolls. If the name wobbles or wavers from the target line, you are not hitting the ball solid. Make sure you use a pendulum motion and stroke through the ball. Practice until you can roll the name straight, then move the ball 3 feet away and begin again.

Drill #43: Coin Toss

Set a ball on the green about 3 feet from the hole. Place a penny under the ball so you cannot see which side of the penny is up. Stroke the ball into the hole, keeping the eyes looking at the ground long enough to see whether the penny is heads or tails. Putt seven or eight balls from this distance. Move back a foot and repeat the drill.

Figure 3.33
Putting swing path.

Drill #44: Control on Short Putts

Stick a tee in the ground about 3 feet from the hole. Place a ball beside the tee, then stick another tee in the ground about 4 inches behind the ball. Putt the ball to the hole without hitting the tee behind it. Putt 6 or 7 more putts from this distance. Move the first tee back 6 feet from the hole, and increase the distance between the ball and the second tee by 3 inches. Repeat the drill. (See Figure 3.34.)

Figure 3.34
Control on short putts.

Figure 3.35

Break line.

Drill #45: Putt to a "T"

Stick a tee in the green and place four balls 2 to 3 feet away. Putt at the tee until you can hit it with each ball. Take one step back and try to hit the tee again. Continue this drill, moving back after you successfully hit the tee with each ball.

Drill #46: Break Line

Place a ball approximately 10 feet from the hole. After determining the break line, place four or five balls along the line between the ball and the hole. Beginning with the ball closest to the hole, putt the ball, concentrating on using a pendulum movement (shoulders, arms, and putter moving as a unit). Continue back along the break line, until all balls are putted. Repeat this drill from various break lines. (See Figure 3.35.)

Drill #47: Putt With Eyes Closed

With the ball approximately 4 to 5 feet from the hole, align putt. Close eyes and putt. Keeping your eyes closed, try to guess if the ball is right or left, long or short of hole. Repeat twice more from the same ball position. Repeat this drill six to seven more times, moving clockwise around the hole. This is an excellent drill for developing a feel for your putt.

Drill #48: Five-In-A-Row

Place five balls in a straight line, starting the first one about 2 feet from the hole and 2 feet between each ball thereafter. Putt the closest ball to the hole, working backward down the line. If you miss a putt, start over. Practice until you make all five balls. (See Figure 3.36.)

Drill #49: Partner Lay-Back

Taking turns with a partner, putt to a hole. If you do not make your putt, move the ball back a putter length from where it stops. Each time you miss, move the ball back, until you hole out. Your partner does the same thing. Play nine holes in this manner. Low score wins.

Figure 3.36

Five in a row.

Drill #50: Wheel Drill

Place ten balls in a circle around the hole, 2 feet away. Work your way around the circle, putting each ball into the hole. If you miss one of the balls, start over. After you can successfully make all putts three consecutive times, move the balls back 2 feet and begin the drill again. (See Figure 3.37.)

Drill #51: Pressure Putts

Place nine balls in a circle around a hole, each about 5 feet from the hole. Start off with 5 points. Every time you make a putt, add 2 points to your score; every time you miss, subtract a point. Get to 10 points and you are a

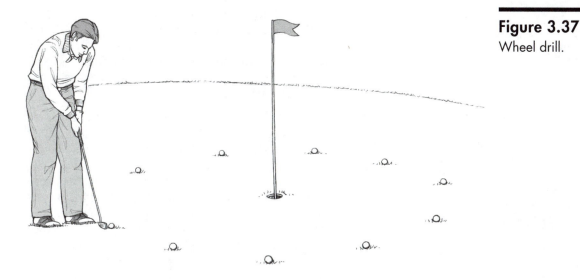

Figure 3.37
Wheel drill.

winner; begin the game again with the balls six feet away from the hole. If you fall to zero, you lose; begin the game again with the balls 4 feet away from the hole. Each time you win or lose, add or subtract another foot accordingly. This drill will prepare you for facing similar pressure putts when on the course.

Drill #52: H-O-R-S-E

This drill is for two or more golfers. The first player decides from which location to putt. If the putt is made, the second player must putt from the same place and make it. If the second player makes the putt, the next player must make it, and so on down the line until someone misses. If the second player misses the putt, he or she gets an "H" and the third player gets to choose a new location to putt from. Each time a player misses, another letter from the word "horse" is added to his or her score. When a player receives an "E," he or she has one chance to retry the putt and erase the letter "E," thereby remaining in the game. If the putt is missed the second time, the player is out of the game. The game continues until only one player is left.

SKILL 3 Trouble Shots

Trouble shots include sand play, uneven lies, play from the rough, and tree shots. Golfers use certain strategies to deal with these.

Sand Play

Sand bunkers are strategically placed throughout most golf courses. You will find them around the greens and along the fairways. By the rules of golf, a sand bunker is considered a hazard, and a player's club must not touch the sand any time during address or backswing.

Greenside Bunker

For most golfers, the greenside sand bunker is the most dreaded place to be on the course. These seemingly innocent areas of sand become vast, relentless wastelands when a ball lands within their boundaries. If a golfer doesn't use

Figure 3.38

Stance in greenside bunker.

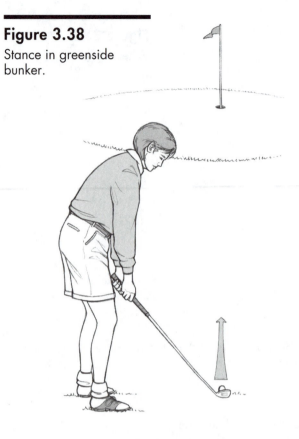

"build a stance" *illegal use of feet to dig out the sand to get a more secure footing*

Figure 3.39

Splash it out.

proper technique to play out of the sand, it may take several attempts before the bunker finally gives up the ball. This can be frustrating and may eventually destroy the golfer's game and his or her confidence as well. Here are some helpful tips to effectively master the greenside bunker shot.

1. *Proper club.* When hitting out of a greenside bunker, use a club that will propel the ball into the air high enough to clear the lip of the trap and land on the green. A sand wedge is the proper club of choice; however, a pitching wedge or 9-iron will suffice if a sand wedge is not available. If you are playing a ball that is buried in the sand, use a pitching wedge, or turn the sand wedge clubface inward to enable the club to get down into the sand. You also might use your pitching wedge or 9-iron when you need to hit the ball a greater distance than a close greenside sand shot.

2. *Length of shot from greenside bunker.* Evaluate the length of the shot from the bunker. Adjust your backswing and followthrough to achieve the necessary distance. For shorter sand shots, a shorter backswing is needed. The longer the shot, the fuller the backswing. A good starting place is to take a backswing and followthrough that are the same length as a pitch shot three times farther away. Keep the length of the followthrough at least as long as the backswing. The only way for you to determine how far the ball will go with variations in the backswing is to practice, practice, practice, until you become familiar with the results.

3. *Stance.* When taking a stance in the sand, make sure your feet are secure, but be careful not to "**build a stance.**" Your stance should be open to target, with the ball opposite the front heel. Your clubface should be open, with the blade aiming at target (see Figure 3.38). If the ball is buried in the sand, play the ball farther back in the stance.

4. *Hitting the ball.* When hitting out of a greenside bunker, make sure the swing path of the club is in the direction of the body alignment, not the club alignment. This will create a slicing action through the sand, enabling the golf club to continue to accelerate rather than decelerate through impact. Do not try to blast, or dig, the ball out of the sand. Rather, "splash it out" (Figure 3.39), concentrating on letting the sand carry it out of the bunker. Take the proper stance, then swing at a point approximately 2 inches behind the ball just as you would at a ball in the fairway. The only difference is that you will not hit the ball; you will hit *behind* the ball. Your objective is to let the sand carry the ball out of the bunker. Take your backswing, accelerate through impact, and end in a balanced finish position. If you have trouble getting the ball high enough, open the clubface more, or swing the club more up than around the body. If you are hitting it too high, close the clubface a little.

Fairway Bunker

Placement of sand bunkers is not limited to the area around the green. Golf courses may have strategically placed bunkers along many fairways to catch errant fairway shots. For beginning golfers, the thought of hitting for distance out of a bunker can be as intimidating as hitting out of a greenside bunker. The following tips will help you develop the necessary tools to become an effective fairway bunker player.

Figure 3.40

Swing in fairway bunker.

1.   *Proper club.* When selecting which club to use, first consider the lie of the ball and the lip of the bunker. If the ball is sitting down in the sand or the bunker has a steep lip, choose a club that has enough loft to get the ball out of the sand and that will assure clearance of the lip. If the ball has a good lie and there is no lip, select the club that will hit the ball the desired distance. A good rule of thumb when hitting a good lie out of a fairway bunker is to use a club that is one club more than the club you would use if the ball were in the fairway. Therefore, if you normally use a 6-iron, use your 5-iron.

2.   *Length of shot.* The backswing and downswing vary little from the normal swing when hitting from a fairway bunker. If the ball is sitting up on the sand, swing just as you would if the ball were in the fairway (see Figure 3.40). If the ball is partially buried in the sand, take a full swing, but bring the clubhead down at a steeper angle in your downswing.

3.   *Stance.* Assume the same stance as you would when hitting a fairway shot, unless you have a buried lie. Make sure your footing is secure; you should not feel unbalanced when swinging. The ball position will vary depending on the loft of the club. Play the ball forward of center of the stance with more lofted clubs, and more toward the center for less lofted clubs. If the ball is buried in the sand, open the stance as you would for a greenside bunker shot to give you a steeper angle of approach (see Figure 3.41).

4.   *Hitting the shot.* Unlike the greenside bunker shot, the fairway bunker shot is hit to create distance. After choosing the correct club and assuming your stance, choke down approximately the same distance the feet have gone down into the sand (see Figure 3.42). Do not bend as much in the knees; keep the legs almost straight. Do not sole or ground the club in the sand, or you will be penalized. The most important thing to remember about the fairway bunker shot is—unlike the greenside bunker shot, where you try to miss the ball and hit the sand—try to hit the ball first.

Anxiety about playing out of sand bunkers comes from not getting enough practice to feel confident about the outcome of your shot. Find a practice bunker, and hit different sand shots until you are familiar with them. Use the drills in this chapter repetitively, and soon you will have increased your awareness of sand shots and skill level to the point that sand bunkers will no longer pose a threat to your game.

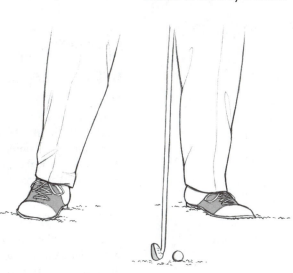

Figure 3.41

Stance in fairway bunker.

Figure 3.42

Hitting from the fairway bunker.

Sand Play Checklist

Greenside Bunkers:

- Relaxed grip
- Blade of club open to target
- Open stance; ball opposite front heel
- Length of backswing relative to distance the ball needs to travel
- Focus on spot 2 inches behind ball, *not the ball.*
- Downswing accelerates through sand to balanced finish

Fairway Bunkers:

- Ball down, steep lip: Choose club with more loft
- Ball up, no lip: Choose club for distance (one club number lower than normal)
- Ball down: Open stance, make swing with steeper angle on downswing
- Ball up: Normal stance, choke down on grip, normal swing
- Use of club with more loft: Position ball forward of center of stance
- Use of club with less loft: Position ball more toward center

Sand-Play Drills

Drill #53: Entry Line

Using the end of the club or the rake handle, draw a straight line 8 to 10 feet long in the sand. Stand at one end of the line. With an open stance, straddle the line so the line is slightly forward of the center of your stance. Swing the club, trying to make the club's point of entry hit the line. Repeat the drill, moving down the line until you reach the other end. When your entry point is consistently on the line, place a ball approximately 2 inches in front of the line and repeat the drill.

Drill #54: Footprint Drill

In a sand bunker, make a footprint where your ball would lie. Set up to the footprint with your sand wedge and make a practice swing, concentrating on trying to erase the entire footprint with the bottom of the club. Do not smash the club into the sand;

Figure 3.43
Footprint drill.

lightly *brush* through the sand. When you can successfully accomplish this, make another footprint and place a ball in the middle of it. Do not focus on the ball; try to make the same swing as before to erase the footprint. Note how your ball will lift out of the bunker as your club slides through the footprint. (See Figure 3.43.)

Drill #55: Out, On, and Close

With 10 balls, see how many balls you can get out of the bunker. When you are able to get 8 of 10 balls out of the bunker, change your goal. See how many you can get *on* the green. Once you are able to get at least 8 balls on the green, attempt to get the balls within a flagstick from the hole.

Drill #56: Sand to Hoop

Beside a practice bunker, place several hoops at various distances from the bunker. Place 10 balls in the sand, then choose one of the hoops as your landing area. Hit each ball out of the sand, trying to land inside the hoop on the first bounce. When you have hit all 10 balls, pick another hoop and begin again. Continue until you have hit into all the hoops. Keep a record of how many balls landed inside each hoop. Each time you perform this drill, try to improve your record until you can successfully land 8 of 10 balls in each landing area.

Drill #57: 21 Points

This is a game for three or more people. The first golfer selects a sand shot to be played and its location. Each person then hits the shot, trying to get closest to the hole. The ball closest to the hole gets 2 points, the next closest gets 1 point, and the farthest away gets no points. If a player makes a hole-in-one, he or she receives 4 points (double the most available points). When the game involves four players, the most available points is 3, with a hole out being worth 6, and with five players, the points go 4–3–2–1, and 8 for a hole-in-one. The first player to reach 21 wins.

Uneven Lies

Although the golf swing is taught and practiced on a level playing field, a level lie is seldom encountered. During a round of golf, a golfer will encounter a variety of stances and ball positions. The four most commonly uneven lies are the uphill lie, downhill lie, ball above feet, and ball below feet. Learning to play the ball from diverse positions is essential to becoming a proficient golfer.

Uphill Lie

pull golf shot that travels straight, but left of the target for right-handers or right of the target for left-handers

underclub hitting with a club that cannot propel the ball the required distance

push golf shot that travels straight, but right of the target for right-handers or left of the target for left-handers

top striking the ball above its horizontal axis

When hitting a ball on an uphill slope, golfers have a tendency to **pull** or **under-club** their shots. To prevent either of these problems from happening, a different set-up to the ball is necessary.

Adjust your weight so the front leg is counterbalancing the gravitational pull toward the back leg and the weight is shifted toward the slope of the hill. Bending more from the knees, particularly the front knee, will aid in accomplishing this shift in weight. The ball position should be played toward the front foot, slightly forward of the middle of the stance. A less lofted club is needed when playing an uphill shot, because the golfer's upward stance will increase the loft of the club. Choking down on the club might be necessary to execute a more controlled swing. After setting up to the ball in this manner (see Figure 3.44), make a normal swing.

Downhill Lie

With a downhill lie, golfers have a tendency to **push** or **top** the ball. To avoid these undesirable shots, flex the back leg to counterbalance the hill angle and shift the body weight toward the slope. Play the ball behind the middle of the stance. The golfer's downward stance will decrease the loft of the club, causing the ball to stay lower to the ground and achieve greater roll. To counteract this, either use a more lofted club with a full swing or take a three-quarter swing with the club you would normally use at that distance. (See Figure 3.45.)

Ball Above Feet

Hooks, pulls, and chunks are a common problem when hitting a ball positioned above the feet. To prevent this, close your stance and shift your weight toward the toes of the feet. Choke down on the club, as the angle of the hill brings the ball higher and closer than normal. Play the ball more toward the center of your stance, and aim to the right of the target, if right-handed, or to the left, if left-handed. The steeper the angle of the hill, the more you will need to adjust your aim. Do not try to hit the ball hard. Instead, use a stronger club and take an easy swing. (See Figure 3.46.)

Ball Below Feet

Of all the uneven lies, hitting a ball that is below the feet is one of the hardest shots to make. Making a few slight adjustments in

Figure 3.44
Uphill lie.

Figure 3.45 (on left)
Downhill lie.

Figure 3.46 (on right)
Ball above feet.

your set-up and alignment can prevent you from topping or pushing the ball—common errors when hitting a ball that is lower than ground level. First, take your stance a little closer to the ball and move your hands up the full length of the grip so the club will be able to reach the ball. Then flex the knees, so you are sitting deeper than normal, and shift your weight more toward your heels to counteract the angle of the hill. Align your shot slightly left of the target if you are right-handed, right of the target if you are left-handed; then take your regular swing. (See Figure 3.47.)

When attempting to hit an uneven lie around the green, the same adjustments should be made as in the full swing shot. Instead of aiming to one side or the other of the target, however, you may want to try opening or closing your clubface to prevent hooking or slicing. Use whichever technique is more effective for you.

Play From the Rough

Golf courses are designed to be played from the fairways, the closely cropped grassy areas leading from the tee to the green. When golfers stray from the fairway into the rough, it becomes more difficult to make solid contact with the ball. When hitting a ball out of the rough, adjustments in set-up, alignment, and swing might be necessary, depending on the lie of the ball.

If the ball is sitting up with a fairly good lie, select one club stronger than you would normally hit from that distance, then address the ball as you normally would and take your regular swing. If the ball is deep in the grass, the grass will get between the clubface and the ball, reducing clubhead speed and closing the clubface. Reduction in speed causes a loss in distance, and a closed clubface will cause the ball to hook. To offset this, open your stance, keeping your clubface pointing at the target, and play the ball slightly forward in your stance. Make the swing path of the club in the direction of the body alignment, not the club alignment, so you are swinging outside to inside, just as in a bunker shot. To get the club on the ball with as little interference as pos-

Figure 3.47
Ball below feet.

sible from the grass, your downswing should be from a steeper angle so you are contacting the ball with a descending blow.

Tree Shots

Trees are everywhere on the golf course. The golfer's likelihood of being behind, under, or against a tree during a round of golf is extremely high. What is the best course of action in these circumstances? The best reaction is to realistically assess the situation *and* your abilities. Golfers who have the most trouble with trees are the ones who try to hit that "magic shot" and end up in worse trouble than when they began. An optimistic old saying goes, "A tree is 90 percent air." Unfortunately, for most of us, it is that 10% of wood that gets us every time. When confronted with a tree shot, consider the following advice for getting the ball back in play.

When your ball is behind a tree, you have several options. If the tree is very close and you are unable to go over it, try hitting underneath the overhanging branches. To do this, you need to keep the ball low, with little backspin, so it will roll. Use a long iron, such as a 3-iron or 4-iron, unless the grass is extremely thick, in which case you might want to hit a 5-iron or 6-iron to get the ball up above the grass. Play the ball slightly on the toe of the club, and swing easy.

If the tree is some distance away, take out a club with plenty of loft to get over it. If the tree is extremely high, open your clubface and play the ball forward in your stance. Take a steep backswing, then hit down and through the ball (see Figure 3.48). Do not try to keep your weight on your back foot during your swing, as you may **scull** the ball or hit it fat.

If you are too close to hit over the tree and the branches are too low to hit under the tree, check for any big gaps in the foliage. To find the right club to hit the ball through the gap, place your iron so the back of the clubhead is on the ground and the shaft is pointing toward the tree. Standing on the clubface, observe where the angle of the shaft is aiming. If it points straight to the gap, this is the club you need to use. This also is a shot you need to practice and feel comfortable with. Consider the risks before attempting this shot. Sometimes it is better to take a middle to short iron and hit the ball into an open area where you will have a clear shot to the green.

scull hitting the top or middle of the ball, resulting in a low trajectory shot that usually goes beyond the intended target

Figure 3.48
Hitting over a tree.

a   Hit down and through.   b   Don't scoop.

If your ball lands under a tree, restricting your swing, take the best course of action. When overhanging branches restrict your backswing, you can't move or break the branches with your hands to improve your position. Many golfers have a tendency to want to take a quick, striking motion to get the ball out. If you try to punch, or snatch at, the ball, you increase your chances of missing the ball.

Practice taking a short backswing, concentrating on swinging smoothly, and try to hit the ball into an open area. If the ball lands close to or up against the wrong side of the tree, disabling your normal swing, try a left-handed shot if you are right-handed, or a right-handed shot if you are left-handed. Using a lofted club or putter, turn the club so the toe is closest to you, then take a short, easy swing, hitting the ball with the back of the toe.

An easier shot is the back-handed shot. Again with your 9-iron or wedge, stand beside the ball, facing away from the target. Holding the club in what is normally your back hand, raise the club and swing downward, keeping the wrist firm and letting the action come from the shoulder.

All of the above-mentioned techniques are viable options and, with practice, can save you a stroke or two. Sometimes, though, the best option is to simply lay out, take a penalty stroke, and drop the ball in a more playable area.

Strategies

Golf is a physical game. Successful golfers must be able to perform complex physical movements, making a small instrument moving at a high rate of speed hit an even smaller object at just the right moment to send it to an intended target. This is not an easy task. Even so, many long-time golfers swear by the old cliché, "Golf is 10 percent physical, 90 percent mental." Although to beginning golfers this may seem to be a highly skewed observation, it is largely based in fact.

Because the outcome of each shot depends primarily on the individual golfer's expertise, he or she alone is responsible for all decisions and actions. There are no coaches, no teammates, no one else to blame if a shot goes awry. For highly skilled players, this can be disconcerting. For less-skilled golfers lacking consistency, this realization can cause much emotional and mental upheaval, interfering with their ability to focus, reason, and deal with the realities of the game and their own performance.

Various psychological strategies can help golfers gain control of their mind and emotions prior to and during play. These, in turn, will improve their overall performance and enjoyment of the game.

PSYCHOLOGICAL STRATEGIES

Avoiding "Paralysis by Analysis"

Beginning golfers often have a difficult time focusing on the shot to be played. Instead, they tend to spend too much time concentrating on the multiple factors of the swing mechanics, worrying about their grip position, arm position, torso position, head position, and so on. Focusing on too many cues can overload the mind and cause more harm than good.

You can almost see some golfers going down a long checklist, trying to make sure they have accomplished each item before beginning the swing. By the time they get to the actual swing, they are unable to relax and swing smoothly and effectively. When beginning golfers step onto the course to play a round of golf, they should have learned the swing fundamentals already. Therefore, their focus should be on the limited steps of the pre-shot routine, not the many intricacies of the swing mechanics.

Mental Imagery

Developing a strong mental routine can help you narrow your focus in much the same way the physical routine does. It is difficult to perform at your best when your mind is wandering, whether you are playing golf or taking a final exam. When playing a golf shot, you need to be able to concentrate 100 percent in the present. Your energy must be focused on the task at hand. Using simple mental cues such as "focus," "back on track," or "think" can be helpful, as can more complex mental images, such as visualizing the shot you are about to make.

When stepping up to the ball, always have a target in mind, and imagine hitting the ball smoothly and solidly. In your mind, picture the desired flight path of the ball to the target and the ball landing in the target area. Most good athletes are able to picture in their mind the skill they are going to execute. This is essential for achieving a high level of performance, whether stepping up to drive a golf ball, performing an intricate offensive play in basketball, or preparing to execute a long tumbling pass during a gymnastics meet. Professionals and amateurs alike need to be able to envision the golf shot before they hit it. Imagery helps overcome the anxiety and uncertainty of the shot, making the actual striking of the golf ball less stressful and more familiar.

Mental imagery is an effective and often forgotten tool for improving physical skills. Research has shown that our bodies tend to follow the direction of our minds. Therefore, clear and correct mental images can aid in concentration and ultimately lead to better scores. For example, some golfers say that pretending the putter is a long pencil with which they are drawing a line away from and then through the ball enables them to make a smooth stroke when putting. Other mental images that golfers use include visualizing a railroad track running from the ball to the hole when putting, imagining a ball in the sand is sitting on a pancake and you want to flip the pancake when hitting out of the sand, and pretending a rope is stretched across in front of you at a certain height and you must pitch the ball over it. Different images work for different individuals. Find what works for you and use it to your advantage.

Self-Confidence

Negative thoughts are detrimental to your game. They gnaw away at your confidence, causing you to become tense and anxious when you set up to your ball. Your swing or your stroke begins to get tight and mechanical, and you begin to lose control over the ball. Loss of control can result in feelings of anger, uncertainty, fear, and frustration. Left unchecked, these negative emotions will ruin your confidence and your golf game.

In contrast, mentally seeing yourself successfully make a good swing and golf shot breeds confidence. Self-confidence enables you to approach any golfing situation with a positive attitude. *What* you concentrate on can directly affect the outcome of your shot. If you are concentrating on the sand traps surrounding the green, more than likely your ball will find its way into one of them. If you are thinking about how close the water hazard is to the hole as you are hitting, your ball will probably get wet.

Put aside any negative thoughts. Instead of thinking, "What if I miss this putt?" visualize the ball going in the hole. Rather than thinking, "I know I'm going to hit into that water hazard running in front of the green," concentrate on the spot where your ball is going to land on the green and imagine the ball rolling up to the hole. The successful golfer stays relaxed and confident, maintaining a positive attitude throughout play, in spite of any difficulties that might arise.

Realistic Expectations

Have you ever watched professional golfers play? They make the game seem effortless, easy. But for many of us, trying to get that small white ball from the tee to the hole on the putting green seems overwhelming. When taking up the game of golf, a person should set *individual* goals. The goals of one golfer may be entirely different from the goals of another. It is important to set goals for yourself that are both short-term *and* long-term, measurable, and attainable. Everyone wants and needs to be able to see progress when working toward a goal. If you set goals that you are unable to reach or are so long-term that you think you will never reach them, you are setting yourself up for failure.

Golf is a game you can't learn to play overnight. The finest PGA Touring Professionals are still learning about and improving their game. Beginning golfers must realize that golf is a game of imperfections. It is not possible to hit every shot perfectly and make every putt. Too many variables can affect the outcome of a round of golf. The intelligent golfer will set realistic goals, allow ample time to develop the necessary golf skills, accept the unpredictability of the game, and play each shot to the best of his or her ability for that day.

Relaxation

Too much tension in the body can wreak havoc in the golf swing. Although muscular contraction is necessary to perform a golf swing, too much muscular tension can interfere with the kinetic chain. Golfers, as well as other athletes, need to learn how to remove that excess tension from the body. Many good relaxation techniques are available. Most are simple and can be done anywhere. Three relaxation techniques are explained briefly here.

ANXIETY / STRESS MANAGEMENT

Stretching

Tension is often a result of overly tight muscles, and stretching will release the tension. A particularly effective stretching exercise is the vertebral roll, often used when warming up before activity. It is an excellent way to stretch the neck, shoulders, and back—integral to the golf swing.

1. Standing with your feet shoulder-width apart and your arms straight, hold a club in your hands so it is resting against the front of the thighs.

2. Concentrating on the position of the vertebral column of your back, begin to roll the body forward by slowly dropping the chin to the chest. Pretend that the head, arms, and club are very heavy, and let them lead the movement.

3. Continue rolling forward, as you *slowly* move the club down the legs toward the ground. Visualize each vertebra of the spine, beginning at the neck, releasing out of line one at a time as the club gets closer to the ground. Let the knees bend slightly, if necessary, to get the club completely on the ground.

4. Hold this position for 10 seconds.

5. Reverse the process. Begin to move each vertebra back into line, starting with the lower back and proceeding upward. Again, concentrate on the heaviness of the head, arms, and club. Let the realignment of the vertebral column pull the club up the legs.

6. Perform this exercise three or four times, along with any other stretching exercises you need for especially tight areas of the body.

Progressive Relaxation

progressive relaxation
the sequential contraction and relaxation of muscle groups in the body

Another proven technique is **progressive relaxation.** When learning to use this method, successful relaxation requires a quiet, comfortable environment without distractions. This technique consists of the tightening and relaxing of muscles starting from the feet and working to the head, or starting at the head and working to the feet. This can be done lying down or sitting in a comfortable chair, whichever position is most comfortable. Each muscle group should be tensed long enough to be noticeable but not long enough to cause cramping or muscle fatigue. When you have contracted and relaxed all the muscle groups, lie or sit quietly. Concentrate on how your body feels without the tension. Try to associate a one- or two-word cue with this feeling, such as "relax," "calm," or "no tension."

After using this technique for a week, omit the contraction phase and concentrate on just relaxing each muscle group, again in sequence. You will begin to be able to consciously relax each muscle group within a few minutes and in other environments. Eventually you will be able to relax the entire body or specific muscle groups while you are in stressful situations, such as competitive tournaments, by simply using your verbal cue.

Rhythmic Breathing

rhythmic breathing
slow, deep inhalations through the nose followed by slow exhalations through the mouth at a specific tempo

There are variations of **rhythmic breathing.** Start with a 4/4 (four counts to inhale, four counts to exhale) or a 4/6 (four counts to inhale, six counts to exhale) rhythm. The key to this technique is to clear the mind of any distractions and focus on the sensation of breathing deep into the abdomen.

When first using this technique, lie on a mat on the floor, or on a firm, yet comfortable, couch or bed. Let your muscles relax and allow the body to become very heavy, as though your body is melting or sinking into the floor or bed. Clear your mind, focusing only on your breathing. Place your hands on your abdomen and feel it rise and fall as you breathe deeply to your chosen tempo. Rhythmic breathing can be done any time and anywhere. It can also be used in combination with stretching or progressive relaxation.

Systematic Desensitization

systematic desensitization method for dealing with pressure situations by practicing potential solutions

Systematic desensitization is often used to relieve anxiety about a given situation. There are many distressing moments on the golf course. How you approach these situations can mean the difference between a good score and a bad score. Finding oneself in an unusually difficult situation during an important golf match can be stressful, particularly if the situation is one that you have not handled well in the past or is unique to anything you have experienced.

The best way to approach potentially unnerving situations is through advance preparation. Defuse possible pressure situations by placing self-imposed imaginary pressures on yourself when practicing. Tell yourself, "I'm on the eighteenth hole, facing a twenty-foot putt for the championship. If I make it, I win a check for one hundred thousand dollars," and then attempt that 20-foot putt.

Participate in competitive partner or group drills that result in only one winner. Plan ahead for potential problem shots you might encounter on the golf course. Visualize possible options to solve these problems, and practice implementing them until you find an appropriate course of action. Then practice, practice, practice, until you can make the necessary shot without anxiety. When the situation arises during actual play, you will be able to approach it with confidence rather than anxiety, with familiarity rather than fear, and your game will benefit from your self-assurance.

Environmental Factors

One reason why golf can be such an enjoyable experience is that it is played in the great outdoors. Ideally, one would like to play under perfect conditions—no wind, no rain, and warm temperatures. Unfortunately, the weather doesn't always cooperate with planned golf outings and can change quickly and unexpectedly. These environmental changes can adversely affect your golf round. Therefore, golfers need to be prepared to deal with unfavorable conditions.

One of the most unpredictable and underestimated environmental factors is wind. Strong winds will test your golfing abilities. If you don't know how to adjust for wind, you will ultimately have to settle for higher sores. The strategy is to get the clubface squarely on the ball, but how do you go about doing that when you are struggling against the wind? The first step before hitting the ball is to notice where the wind is blowing. Will you be hitting downwind, into a headwind, or against a crosswind? The direction of the wind will determine how you need to approach your shot.

Downwind

Because the wind is blowing toward the hole, the ball will stay in the air longer than usual. Take advantage of this by hitting the ball higher and harder, to give yourself more length off the tee. Widen your stance to give yourself a more balanced base and to shorten your swing. Try hitting less club, such as a 3-wood or 4-wood instead of a driver, or a 5-iron instead of a 3-iron, to give you more control over the shot and greater loft. Or stand more behind the ball to get that added height.

The higher trajectory will get the ball up into the wind, increasing the distance the ball will carry and reducing the backspin. Take this into consideration when hitting approach shots into the green with the wind behind you. To prevent the ball from overreaching the target, you may want to play your ball short of the green and let it bounce and roll, or you may need to open your clubface a little, slow down your swing, and drop the ball softly onto the green.

Headwind

A common error when hitting into a wind is to rush the swing, trying to hit the ball harder to force it through the wind. Adjustments should be made in stance and ball position rather than swing rhythm. When hitting from the teebox, do not tee the ball too low. Typical advice is to tee the ball down to keep the ball low. Although this is a seemingly sensible suggestion, following this advice most often results in unsolid hits.

Instead, set up to the ball with more weight on your front foot, again widening your stance. Place the ball farther back in your stance and slightly closer to your body, then try to swing through the ball. This club position will provide less loft on the club face, keeping the ball lower.

When hitting irons against a headwind, equalize the tilt of the shoulders by lowering your front shoulder and raising your back shoulder on address. Play the ball back in your stance, even as far back as your back foot when hitting a short iron. Using the top of the flag as your target, select a club that is one to two clubs stronger that you would normally hit, depending on the force of the wind. Choking down on the club 1 to 2 inches, take a 3/4 length backswing and swing with your normal rhythm. When pitching into a headwind with a lofted club, try to land the ball close to the hole, as the ball will stop quickly. Or, instead of pitching the ball, use a chip shot to keep the ball low.

Crosswind

slice wind a wind blowing left to right (right-handers) or right to left (left-handers)

hook wind a wind blowing right to left (right-handers) or left to right (left-handers)

When the wind is blowing across the fairway (see Figure 4.1), use it to your advantage. When playing against a **slice wind**, set your weight toward your heels and aim down the side of the hole the wind is blowing from. If the fairway slopes in the direction the wind is blowing, aim a little farther up the slope, even out into the rough, if necessary. If it is a **hook wind**, set your weight more toward your toes and aim down the side of the hole the wind is blowing from. The ball will land and roll at an angle finishing in the middle of the fairway. Also, if you naturally slice or hook the ball, the wind will double the effects, so make appropriate adjustments in your alignment.

Other Environmental Factors

Other factors that must be considered include rain, cold temperatures, and hot, humid weather. Being prepared means dressing appropriately and carrying the proper equipment in your golf bag.

Figure 4.1

Hitting into a crosswind.

Never play golf during a storm. If you see lightening, even at a great distance, discontinue play and seek shelter until the storm is over.

When playing in rain not associated with a thunder and lightening storm, a good rain suit and an umbrella large enough to cover yourself and your golf bag during rain play are essential, as are several dry towels and some spare golf gloves in case the one you are wearing gets wet. One of the most common problems associated with rain is losing control of the club because of a wet grip. A golf bag rain cover will help keep grips dry by preventing rain from getting in the bag.

During cold weather, proper clothing is critical. Wear clothing that can be layered, yet allows some freedom of movement. Long underwear, a turtleneck, a loose sweater, and heavy pants are good choices. Keeping your head, hands, and feet warm and dry is a priority. A winter cap, golf mittens, cool-weather gloves, several layers of socks, and waterproof shoes are integral items of apparel for cold weather.

When playing in hot temperatures, golfers need to be wary of becoming overheated and getting sunburned. Wearing light-colored clothing and a visor or hat will help the golfer stay cool. Also, keep a damp, cool towel on your bag or in the golf cart. Protect exposed areas of skin with sunblock, wear sunglasses, and drink plenty of water when you are out in the sun for long periods. Humidity will make golfers perspire more, so make sure you have several dry towels and spare golf gloves in your bag to keep your hands and grip dry.

Glossary

aerobic exercise rhythmical large-muscle activity of moderate intensity performed for at least 20 minutes without interruption

all square having won an equal number of holes as the competition during match play

approach shot stroke made with the intent of having the ball finish on the green

balata synthetic form of the dried, green-like juice from a West Indian tree

ball marks small indentations on the putting surface made by a ball hit into the green

birdie one stroke under par

bogey one stroke over par

"build a stance" illegal use of feet to dig out the sand to get a more secure footing

boundaries outer perimeter of golf course beyond which play is not allowed

casting starting the downswing with the arms

compression relative hardness of the golf ball

divots pieces of sod cut by a clubhead during a swing

double bogey two strokes over par

double eagle three strokes under par

eagle two strokes under par

fairway closely mowed playing area between the tee and the green

fringe grass surrounding the green that is shorter than the fairway but longer than the green

grain direction the blades of grass grow and lie on the green

green closely mowed area of a golf course that contains the hole, cup, and flagstick

handicap average number of strokes a player's score is over par

hole-in-one ball is hit into the hole from the teeing ground in one stroke

holes up having won more holes than the competition during match play

honors the privilege of hitting first

hook golf shot that curves from right-to-left for right-handers or left-to-right for left-handers

hook wind a wind blowing right-to-left (for right-handers) or left-to-right (for left-handers)

interlock position grip position in which the last finger of the back hand interlocks the first finger of the target hand

kinetic chain energy-creating sequence of movements that are each a result of preceding actions

line the direction the ball will take when putted

loft the degree the clubface angles from the vertical plane

mark to place a small object, preferably a coin or plastic marker, behind the golf ball

match play a competition between golfers, the winner of which is determined by who wins the most holes

offset putter a putter whose putting blade is behind the shaft of the putter

par number of strokes that an expert golfer is expected to make for a given hole

progressive muscular relaxation the sequential contraction and relaxation of muscle groups in the body

provisional ball a second ball hit from the original position of a ball that is thought to be out-of-bounds or lost

pull golf shot that travels straight but left of the target for right-handers and right of the target for left-handers

push golf shot that travels straight but right of the target for right-handers and left of the target for left-handers

putter vertical-faced club used to roll the ball into the hole on the green

repetition number of times the exercise is performed

rhythmic breathing slow, deep inhalations through the nose followed by slow exhalations through the mouth at a specific tempo

rough grassy area skirting the fairway that is less manicured than the fairway

sand bunker hazard filled with sand within the boundaries of the golf course

scull to hit the top or middle of the ball, resulting in a low trajectory shot that usually goes beyond the intended target

set a group of repetitions

slice golf shot that curves from left-to-right for right-handers or right-to-left for left-handers

slice wind a wind blowing left-to-right (for right-handers) or right-to-left (for left-handers)

stance position of the feet when the player addresses the ball

static stretch a slow, sustained stretch to the point where the body feels a resistive tension, followed by several seconds of relaxation while holding the stretch

stretch reflex an involuntary muscle contraction in response to sudden, potentially harmful extension of the muscle

stroke-and-distance penalty penalty stroke given when the ball is lost, hit out-of-bounds, or hit in a water hazard, and the player puts another ball into play from where the ball was last hit

stroke play a competition between golfers, the winner of which is determined by who completes the round with the fewest strokes

Surlyn® hard, cut-resistant material made by the DuPont Company, as a covering for golf balls

swingweight the total weight of the club multiplied by the distance from a specified point from the grip end—12 to 14 inches, depending on the scale—to the point at which the golf club balances

systematic desensitization method for dealing with pressure situations by practicing potential solutions

tee wooden or plastic peg on which the ball is placed

teeing ground designated starting place for each hole

ten-finger position grip position in which all fingers on both hands wrap around the club; also known as the baseball grip

top striking the ball above its horizontal axis

trajectory the path of the ball through the air

triple bogey three strokes over par

underclub hitting with a club that cannot propel the ball the required distance

up and down finishing the hole with one chip or pitch and one putt

Vardon overlapping grip grip position in which the last finger of the back hand overlaps the first finger of the target hand

water hazard water obstacle on golf course defined by red or yellow stakes/lines

Index